IMAGES
of America

THE BEDFORD SPRINGS HOTEL

The Bedford Springs Hotel's stagecoach sits in front of the main building while it waits to take guests on an excursion in this c. 1892 photograph. The excursions were called "Tally Ho" parties and occurred quite frequently at the resort. Dressed for an evening out, the visitors seen in this photograph are probably going to the nearby Willows for one of its famous chicken dinners. (Courtesy of the Bedford Springs Historical Society.)

ON THE COVER: Throughout its history, the Bedford Springs Hotel attracted wealthy and influential patrons, personified by the four well-dressed and dignified-looking gentlemen in this c. 1880 photograph. Although they probably came to the resort for rest and relaxation, there is no doubt that they discussed business concerns—perhaps steel prices or railroad construction—as they sat nonchalantly on the broad lawn in front of the hotel buildings. Unfortunately, their identities are not known, but it is possible that they are Pittsburgh industrialists. (Courtesy of the Bedford Springs Historical Society.)

IMAGES
of America

THE BEDFORD SPRINGS HOTEL

Alison Reed Ross

ARCADIA
PUBLISHING

ISBN 978-0-7385-9298-5

Published by Arcadia Publishing
Charleston, South Carolina

Printed in the United States of America

Library of Congress Control Number: 2012937255

For all general information, please contact Arcadia Publishing:
Telephone 843-853-2070
Fax 843-853-0044
E-mail sales@arcadiapublishing.com
For customer service and orders:
Toll-Free 1-888-313-2665

Visit us on the Internet at www.arcadiapublishing.com

This book is dedicated to my parents, Dave and Norma Reed, for the constant support and love they have shown me throughout my life.

CONTENTS

Acknowledgments

"What has been will be again, what has been done will be done again; there is nothing new under the sun," wrote King Solomon, and so it is with the topic of the Bedford Springs Hotel. Much has been written by a number of people about the venerated hotel and its history. Well-researched and lovingly written books have been prepared by others before me, such as William L. Defibaugh, PE; Jon Baughman; Ned Frear; and Daniel L. Burns.

In approaching this project, I did not want to try to supersede the work of others, for each person's work stands on its own. Instead, this volume presents a different format, mostly a pictorial one, presenting the resort's development and the people and events that shaped its history. My search for additional information led me to the Bedford County Historical Society, the Pennsylvania State Archives and the Pennsylvania State Library in Harrisburg, and the College of Physicians in Philadelphia.

My heartfelt thanks go to William L. Defibaugh, PE, who has spent many years preserving the legacy of the Bedford Springs Hotel and establishing the Bedford Springs Historical Society. Through Bill's generosity and graciousness, I was able to access the images in the society's collection and the information in his book *The First Days of the Bedford Springs*. The following people also assisted with this project: Jim Nagle of Forse Design Inc.; Cliff Saxton Jr. and the White Sulphur Springs Museum and Archives; Mark F. Heiman of Loomis House Press in Northfield, Minnesota; Steve Long of the Doubling Gap Center in Newville, Pennsylvania; the Spanierman Gallery, LLC, in New York City; and the Tufts Archives at the Pinehurst History Museum in Pinehurst, North Carolina.

Thanks also go to my parents, Dave and Norma Reed, and to my husband, Jim Ross, for their support and encouragement; to Germaine Germeyer and Alan Beauregard for their support and editorial comments; and to my acquisitions editor, Abby Henry, for her enthusiasm and attentiveness.

Care has been taken to present accurate information, and any errors are unintentional. For additional information on the Bedford Springs Hotel, it is hoped that readers will refer to the informative books by the authors listed above. Unless otherwise noted, the images in this book are from the Bedford Springs Historical Society.

INTRODUCTION

When Dr. John Anderson first established his mineral springs spa in 1796 on his property near Bedford, Pennsylvania, he probably had no idea how successful, enduring, and venerated the resort would become.

The Bedford Springs Hotel is located in Bedford County in western Pennsylvania, north of the Maryland-Pennsylvania state line. Bedford County was formed from the larger Cumberland County by an act of the Colonial legislature in March 1771. Still quite large at the time, Bedford County extended westward to the Ohio border and earned the nickname "Mother Bedford."

The town of Bedford evolved from a small trading post that had been established in the 1750s by Robert Ray on the South Branch of the Juniata River. Growing into one of a number of important camps on Pennsylvania's western frontier, it was known by several names, including the Camp at Rays Town, Camp Raystown, and Camp Racetown. By 1758, provincial soldiers occupied the camp, and a fort was constructed. It became known as Fort Bedford, after the Duke of Bedford in Bedfordshire, England.

In 1766, William Penn's sons Thomas and Richard Penn laid out an adjacent town and named it after the fort. Bedford's advantageous location along the well-traveled Forbes Road, which extended from Philadelphia to Pittsburgh, as well as its beautiful, fertile land enabled it to grow quickly. On March 13, 1795, Bedford was incorporated as a borough by an act of the state legislature.

The development of a mineral springs spa resort south of Bedford began in the 1790s during an exciting time in both Pennsylvania and the new republic of the United States of America. In 1794, during the Whiskey Rebellion, Pres. George Washington led a military expedition to western Pennsylvania and stayed in the town of Bedford, using the Espy House as his headquarters. The trip was notable because it was the first and only time an American president led troops in the field while in office.

In Pennsylvania as well as the new nation, opportunities abounded for the adventurous in spirit and enterprise, and farmers, businessmen, and professionals set out toward the frontier to start new lives for themselves and their families. Many who were educated in eastern cities moved westward, utilizing their influence to establish themselves in growing Pennsylvania towns, such as Carlisle, Shippensburg, and Bedford. Dr. John Anderson, the developer of the Bedford Springs spa resort, belonged to this group and used his ingenuity, influence, and family ties to become one of the most successful businessmen in Bedford.

The immediate success of the mineral springs spa at Bedford was fueled by events occurring nationally at the time. The first buildings at the spa were completed in 1804, the same year as the start of Lewis and Clark's wilderness expedition. The sense of curiosity, exploration, and discovery that pervaded the country's imagination affected those closer to home, prompting them to travel to places like the Bedford Springs to make their own discoveries.

The desire for optimal health was no different 200 years ago than it is today. Americans wanted cures for their rheumatism, digestive issues, and stress and traveled great distances to find new treatments. By the middle of the 1700s, American colonists had already been traveling to other mineral springs to "take the waters." The springs at what is now Berkeley, West Virginia, were depicted as the "Medicine Springs" as early as 1747. First named the Town of Bath after the famous

English spa town, Berkeley Springs became well known and has remained a spa destination to this day. The establishment of mineral spring spas in Pennsylvania was not far behind. The Chalybeate Springs Hotel in Bedford, the White Sulphur Springs Hotel in Milligan's Cove (near Bedford), and the Doubling Gap White Sulphur Springs Hotel in Newville, Cumberland County, joined Bedford Springs as popular mineral spring destinations.

Pennsylvania and West Virginia were not the only locales where spring resorts were established. By the 1860s, resorts had developed at natural springs throughout the country as the benefits of hydrotherapy, by then a serious science, were increasingly touted. Guidebooks to spas throughout the country were written by leading practitioners of hydrotherapy, including Dr. John J. Moorman and Dr. William F. Fitch. The doctors described the mineral springs at each of the resorts, including Bedford Springs, and the chemical composition of the water at each spring. The guidebooks also described the internal and external water therapies available at the resorts. Balneology, the science of using baths for therapeutic effects, was highly regarded and a major selling point for the Bedford Springs Hotel.

The success of the early Bedford Springs Hotel also depended on the transportation network across Pennsylvania. The establishment of the first through line of stagecoaches from Philadelphia to Pittsburgh occurred in 1804, the same time as the opening of Doctor Anderson's mineral springs spa, and provided transportation for distant travelers. The development of a continuous turnpike across Pennsylvania soon followed with the 1815 establishment of five connecting turnpike companies between Philadelphia and Pittsburgh: the Harrisburg, Carlisle, and Chambersburg; the Chambersburg and Bedford; the Bedford and Stoyestown; the Stoyestown and Greensburg; and the Greensburg and Pittsburgh turnpike companies.

In 1854, the Pennsylvania Railroad Company completed a continuous rail line from Philadelphia to Pittsburgh, promoting an increase in travel across Pennsylvania and providing easier access to the Bedford region. The Baltimore & Ohio Railroad ran a line to Bedford from Cumberland, Maryland, as well. In the latter half of the 19th century, travel by railroad made mineral springs resorts more accessible to more people, democratizing travel for the American public like never before. By the 1890s, a new class of resort traveler joined the elite politicians and members of the upper class at the spa resorts. Well-to-do families with industrial-era fortunes arrived from Pittsburgh, Baltimore, York, and Philadelphia and signed their names on the guest registers.

By the middle of the 19th century, a transition had started to occur, and the science of hydrotherapy began to play less of a role in attracting visitors to the resorts. Spa resorts were frequented less for the therapeutic benefits of their waters and more for their lively social scenes. The Bedford Springs Hotel exemplified this trend, and by the 1890s, it had become as popular a destination as Saratoga Springs in upstate New York and the White Sulphur Springs Hotel in Greenbrier County, West Virginia.

The 1895 construction of Bedford Springs's golf course, one of the first in America, drew vacationers during that decade and into the 20th century, this time in their new automobiles. After struggling to survive during the Great Depression, the resort faced a new set of challenges during World War II. In 1942, the hotel was used by the US government as a naval training school for radiomen, and in 1945, the hotel suddenly became an internment facility for detained Japanese diplomats. Following the war, the hotel was extensively renovated and opened its doors again to receive vacationers during a modern era of tourism. The hotel remained an upscale year-round resort and golf course for the next 40 years. After straining to stay profitable through uncertain economic times in the late 1970s and 1980s, the Bedford Springs Hotel was finally forced to close its doors in 1987.

On December 20, 1984, the Bedford Springs Hotel Historic District was added to the National Register of Historic Places, and on July 17, 1991, the hotel property was designated a National Historic Landmark, the highest designation a historic property can receive The hotel's new owners undertook a $120 million renovation, expansion, and golf course restoration between 2005 and 2007. When the ambitious project was finished, the Bedford Springs Hotel opened its doors again as the beautiful Bedford Springs Omni Resort.

One

Developing the Spa

For years, the Bedford region has been celebrated for its natural beauty. In an 1860 guidebook to American and Canadian mineral springs, Bedford was described as a region noted for its "pure invigorating air, salubrious climate, and beautiful and varied scenery." This view of the Bedford area was painted by German artist Augustus Kollner in 1840. (Courtesy of the Spanierman Gallery, LLC, New York.)

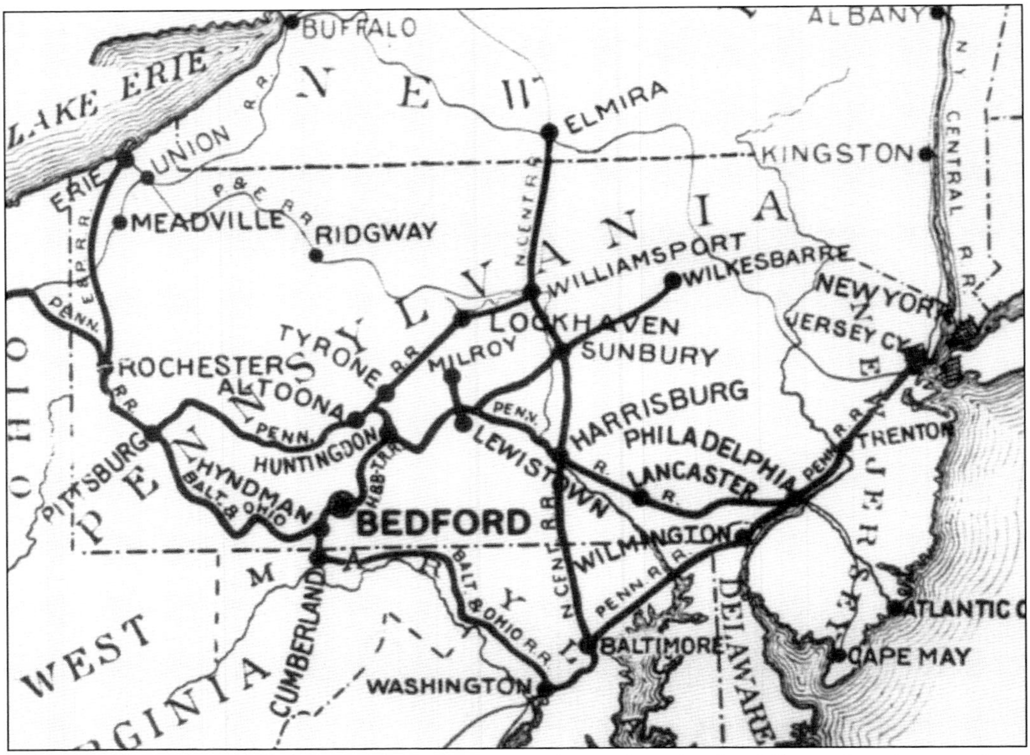

Bedford County is in southwestern Pennsylvania above the Maryland-Pennsylvania state line. The Allegheny Mountains cross the county in a southwest to northeast direction, and the town of Bedford lies in a valley of the South Branch of the Juniata River. This 1902 map shows the location of Bedford in relation to other Pennsylvania cities.

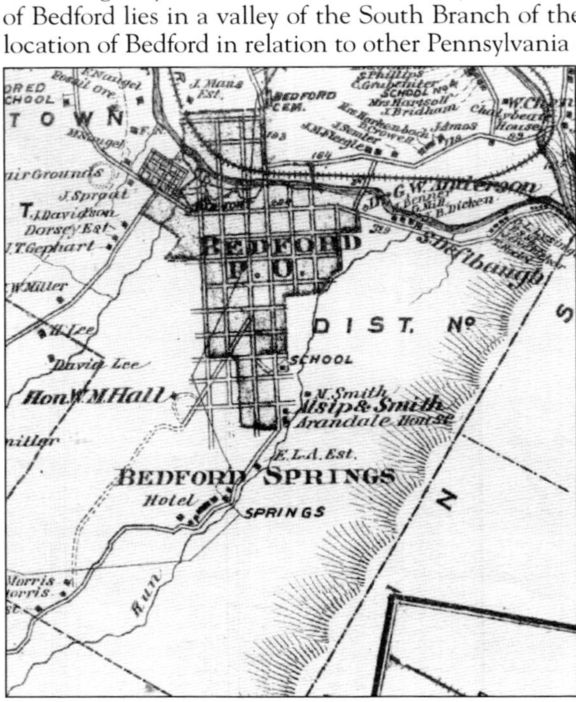

The road leading to the mineral springs originated as a path used by Native Americans. The path started at Ray's Trading Post on the South Branch of the Juniata River. It extended southwest from the settlement through a 150-foot-wide valley between two mountains known as Federal Hill and Constitution Hill. The road is shown alongside Shober's Run in this 1888 map of Bedford and its surroundings. (Courtesy of the Pennsylvania State Library.)

Centuries before European settlers arrived in the Bedford area and "discovered" the medicinal qualities of the water, the springs were widely known to the region's Native Americans. Legends describe a "medicinal spring" to which Tuscarora, Shawnee, and Iroquois tribes traveled from distant locations to take advantage of the healing powers of the waters. The area around the medicinal springs was consecrated as neutral ground for gatherings and meetings. Wounded and sick people came to the springs to drink the water to cure their ills. Settlers around Fort Bedford knew about the Native American activity at the mineral springs. At first, they thought that the springs were used by the tribes just as a temporary watering and resting place, but they soon heard about the healing powers of the water.

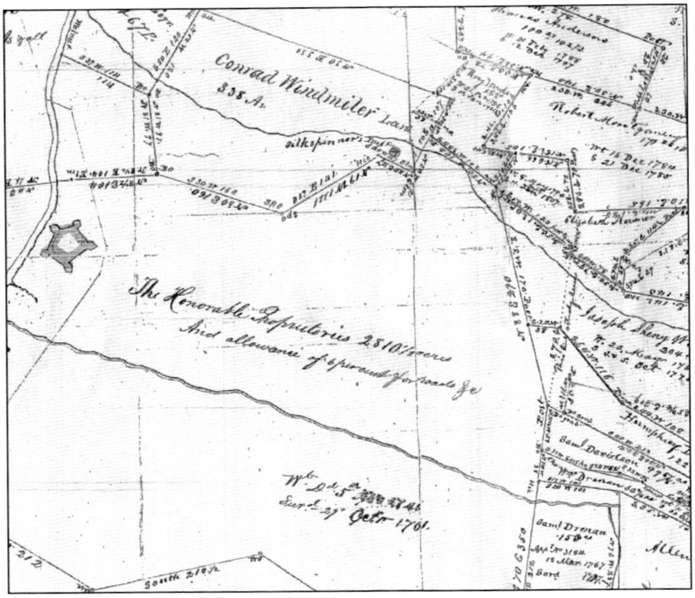

By 1758, local resident Joseph Sheniwolf owned 204 acres of land in the valley and had constructed a building on the property. Sheniwolf's tract included the land where the golf course is now located as well as three of the mineral springs. Adjacent to his parcel was a large tract owned by the Penn family, the "Honorable Proprietories." This undated map shows Fort Bedford on the map's left and Sheniwolf's property toward the right.

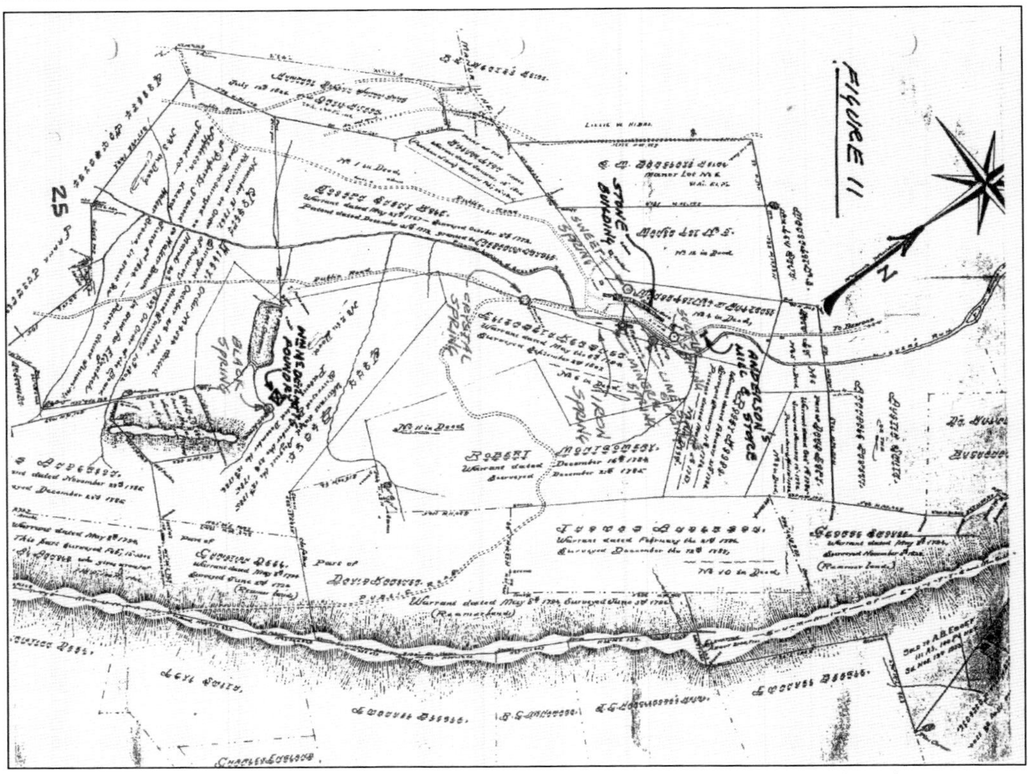

Sheniwolf is believed to have been a Native American from the Tuscarora tribe whose parents purchased property from the provincial government and converted to Christianity. Sheniwolf obtained a warrant in 1767 and tried to sell the land to Samuel Findley. The sale did not occur, and Sheniwolf later sold it to Frederick Naugle in 1772. Above is a c. 1900 map showing early land ownership in the area.

One of the earliest settlers in the Bedford area was Thomas Anderson, who came from Ireland in 1766 and settled at Fort Bedford. Thomas's second son, John Anderson, was born in 1770. As a boy, John became familiar with the mineral springs south of town. He went to Dickinson College in Carlisle, Pennsylvania, where he majored in medicine and studied law as a minor. He also studied medicine in Philadelphia under Dr. William Shippen, an anatomy professor at the University of Pennsylvania. Doctor Shippen stated in a February 3, 1791, letter that Anderson "has attended my course of lectures on anatomy surgery and midwifery with great care and diligence." Dr. John Anderson returned to Bedford and married Mary Espy, daughter of Capt. David Espy and granddaughter of George Woods, a justice of King George III. (Courtesy of the Pennsylvania State Library.)

This photograph depicts a cabin on the mill property. In Frederick Naugle's 1775 will, he requested that one third of the money from the sale of his plantation and mill on Shober's Run be left to his wife. In 1787, when he was just 17 years old, John Anderson was the low bidder at an auction where he acquired 100 acres of land on the "Mill Tract." Apparently, he was quite aware of the value of the land there.

After his return from studying medicine in Philadelphia, Dr. John Anderson purchased the remaining springs property in 1796 and proceeded with his plans to develop the spa. He used the spring's medicinal waters to treat his patients, and the mill building (pictured) was used as both a store and a doctor's office.

Doctor Anderson soon started improving the property by cleaning out the springs. He then constructed temporary bathhouses, small boardinghouses, and bathing facilities with hot and cold mineral water in in-ground tubs. With the help of local residents and tradesmen, Anderson built the first hotel building between 1803 and 1804 west of Shober's Run, as seen in this watercolor painted by Augustus Kollner in 1840. (Courtesy of the Spanierman Gallery, LLC, New York.)

Constructed of limestone from Federal Hill, the building stood two and a half stories tall, was 12,000 square feet in area, and had 24 guest rooms. The hotel was four times the size of the largest inn in town and boasted a sizable kitchen with a cooking fireplace, a dining room, a living room, a drawing room, and a lobby. This is an 1817 image showing the Stone House, as it was known, on the far right and the Crockford Building in the center.

CROCKFORD, BACHELORS' QUARTERS, BEDFORD SPRINGS

The spa resort was successful, and by 1811, Doctor Anderson had begun adding to the accommodations. He constructed the first portion of the bachelors' quarters, known as the Crockford Building, on property west of the stream near the Stone House. The new building housed bachelors and families, while the original stone building was reserved for ladies and their families. This c. 1870 photograph is of the Crockford Building.

In his 1809 journal, Joshua Gilpin reported that Doctor Anderson had built a handsome and large frame house and several smaller ones for families. He declared that of all watering places in America that he had seen, this was the most worthy to be visited. This is another photograph (date unknown) of the Crockford Building.

People were excited about the "newly discovered" springs at Bedford. According to the December 20, 1803, *Lancaster Journal*, four springs existed at the resort: the Sulphur Spring, the Yellow Spring, the Moss Spring, and another spring that remained unnamed. People could drink the water or bathe in it, and it acted immediately and powerfully as a "Diuretic and a Cathartic." The women in this c. 1890 photograph are shown visiting the magnesia spring.

A later invitation by Rev. R. Weiser of Bedford County states, "Let those who are afflicted come to this beautiful and romantic spot, and have their debilitated constitutions strengthened and invigorated—let them inhale our pure, bracing, and salubrious air, and drink from our gushing fountain of health, and the trembling limbs will soon become firm." This c. 1900 photograph shows Shober's Run, into which several of the mineral springs flowed.

Hundreds of people started coming to the springs, and there was soon a shortage of hotel accommodations. People either camped on the grounds or stayed at the inns in town. When the hotels were full, visitors had to stay outside of town at the inns of George Funk, Jacob Bonnet, and John Defibaugh. This is a photograph of the still extant Jean Bonnet Tavern. (Courtesy of the Library of Congress.)

The Defibaugh Tavern, located three miles east of the springs, had a special relationship with the Bedford Springs Hotel throughout its history. John Defibaugh opened his inn in 1774, and, as evidenced by store ledgers, he purchased many of his restaurant supplies from Anderson's mill. Many of Doctor Anderson's guests stayed at Defibaugh's tavern while the hotel was under construction. This c. 1890 photograph shows hotel guests visiting the Defibaugh Tavern.

In 1825, Doctor Anderson expanded the hotel again by constructing an addition to the Crockford Building, and in 1830, he constructed the first Evitt Building south of the Stone House. Solomon Filler was apparently the builder and constructed a two-and-a-half story frame building measuring 130 feet in length. It contained 22 additional guest rooms, an elegant drawing room, and a large dining room. Filler renovated the springs and bathing facilities—including the addition of benches for the iron springs; a new bridge, stairs, and railings; a new steam tub; and more tubs and troughs. He repaired pumps, the shower baths, the reservoir, the warm bathhouse, and the fence surrounding the fountain. A stable and barn were also constructed. This is a c. 1890 photograph of the Evitt Building as it was being enlarged.

By 1824, the Bedford Springs Hotel was famous. A newspaper called the *National Gazette and Literary Register* called the hotel the "Montpelier of America," with its music, nightly balls, billiards, quoits, and bowling. The hotel served mountain mutton and venison and carefully selected wines and liquors. The best musicians and servants were hired to work at the hotel. By 1835, the spa was selling lifelong memberships, also called life tickets. When men worked for John Anderson, they requested life tickets for $10 each. By that time, over 200 people had life tickets. There were 34 men—original contributors to the spa—who were entitled to lifetime use of the spa. This drawing by artist Kevin Klutz is of a statue of Hygeia, the goddess of health, that was installed on the front lawn in approximately 1830.

Two

TAKING THE WATERS

The mid-19th century was a prosperous time for Bedford Springs. After Doctor Anderson's death in 1839, his children continued to expand the resort with additional hotel buildings. Its mineral water was well known, and the family established a thriving water-bottling business on the property. The hotel's amenities and the area's natural beauty attracted visitors from near and far. Shown here is the Colonial Building, which soon became the resort's centerpiece.

Before the Pennsylvania Railroad system was completed across the state, travel to Bedford Springs was still primarily by stagecoach. In 1819, a four-horse stage from Philadelphia took 60 hours and cost $18. After arriving at Bedford, people traveled down to the springs in a two- or four-seated hack. This 1840 watercolor by Augustus Kollner depicts travelers near Bedford. (Courtesy of the Spanierman Gallery, LLC, New York.)

This 1840 watercolor by Augustus Kollner depicts the town of Bedford, which was highly praised by author I. Daniel Rupp in his 1848 history of Bedford County. He exclaims, "As you approach the summit of the hill, Bedford bursts into view. The spot on which it stands seems to have been scooped out of the mountains by the hands of God." (Private collection, courtesy of the Spanierman Gallery, LLC, New York.)

From 1838 to 1842, the Anderson heirs constructed the Colonial Building in the Greek Revival style of architecture. Erected by Solomon Filler, the large brick masonry building was imposing and impressive, with Doric-style columns that measured 23 feet in height and walls that were five bricks thick. A well-dressed gentleman is seen in front of the building in this dramatic c. 1860 photograph.

Another structure was built in 1838 south of the Colonial Building. It housed the kitchen, bowling, and billiards. This c. 1860 photograph depicts the hotel buildings from the south, with the kitchen building on the left, the Colonial Building in the center, and the Crockford Building on the right.

Bedford Springs continued to expand, and a new stone and wood-frame building, known as the Swiss Building, was constructed on the property, as seen in this c. 1890 photograph. The new building was attached to the Stone House to the north. Construction took just two months—from November 1856 to January 1857. The stone foundation was excavated and laid, followed by the building of the frame structure.

This postcard shows the Swiss Building as viewed from the northeast, with the renovated Stone House to the left. The new building included baths that were located in the basement. The road in front of the hotel was graded, and stone culverts were built. By this time, the resort occupied 1,600 acres of land.

NORTH WING BEDFORD SPRINGS HOTEL

This c. 1870 photograph depicts the decorative wooden gate installed on the hotel's front lawn to accentuate the resort's entrance. The image shows that the front of the hotel was fully developed, with curved stone masonry planters on each side of the entrance gate, a circular drive leading to the front of the Colonial Building, a landscaped lawn with planting beds, and shade trees.

In 1850, a new staircase and bridge crossing the creek were constructed. They were tied into a stone masonry wall that fronted the hotel property. The staircase's balustrade and posts matched the classical architecture of the hotel's Colonial Building. In this c. 1880s photograph, a wagon and its drivers have stopped in front of the staircase, waiting to give guests a ride.

Another staircase and bridge, much grander than the previous ones, were built in 1880. By this time, the hotel's front lawn was improved with decorative and festive-looking wooden gates and fencing in the prevailing style of resort architecture and were painted to match the hotel's porches. This c. 1890 photograph shows a family posing on the new stairway.

The hotel was redecorated in 1857, and new chairs, carpeting, and wallpaper were purchased. Frescoes were painted onto the walls of the dining room, entrance hall, and staircase. A drastic change to the hotel was the painting, or "colouring," of parts of the hotel's porch to a darker color to match the prevailing Victorian style. This print shows the property as it must have appeared in 1861.

This modern-day collage by artist Kevin Klutz depicts many different scenes of the hotel and grounds, including the newly added wooden gazebos, gates, and fencing on the front lawn.

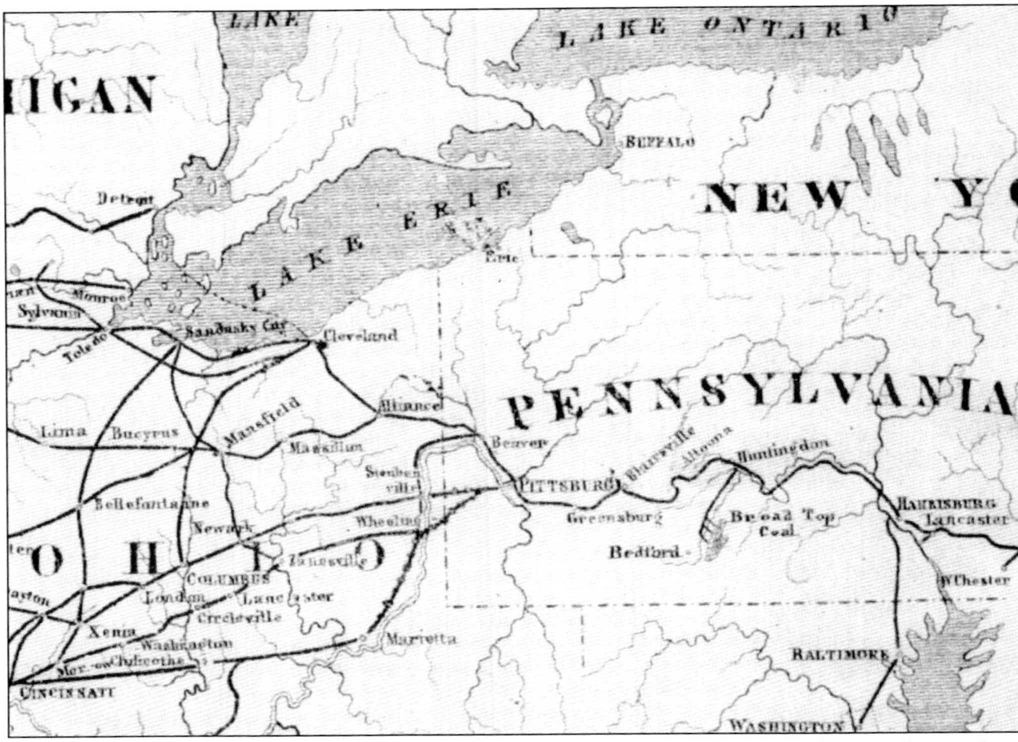

The Pennsylvania Railroad Company completed its route across the state of Pennsylvania from Philadelphia to Pittsburgh in 1854, making travel to Bedford easier and faster. A traveler going to Bedford would get off at Huntingdon and transfer onto a short-line railroad used primarily for carrying coal, the Huntingdon & Broad Top Mountain Railroad, to get to the Bedford vicinity. This 1857 Pennsylvania Railroad Company map shows the railroad line across the state.

The Bedford Railroad Depot was built in approximately 1872 when the Bedford Division of the Pennsylvania Railroad was established. This c. 1880 photograph shows a stagecoach and a wagon that are waiting by the rails for the arrival of the train.

This c. 1890 photograph shows departing travelers at the Bedford Railroad Depot. Visitors were transported between the hotel and train station twice a day in a wagon and later a stagecoach.

Starting in 1858, travelers from Washington, DC, could take the Baltimore & Ohio Railroad to Cumberland, Maryland. From Cumberland, stagecoaches left for Bedford Springs every morning at 6:00 a.m. The 23-mile ride took half a day, and guests arrived at the hotel in time for supper. The entire trip cost $7.75. This Baltimore & Ohio map shows Bedford Springs near the top of the map, below the title. (Courtesy of the Woodbridge [New Jersey] Public Library.)

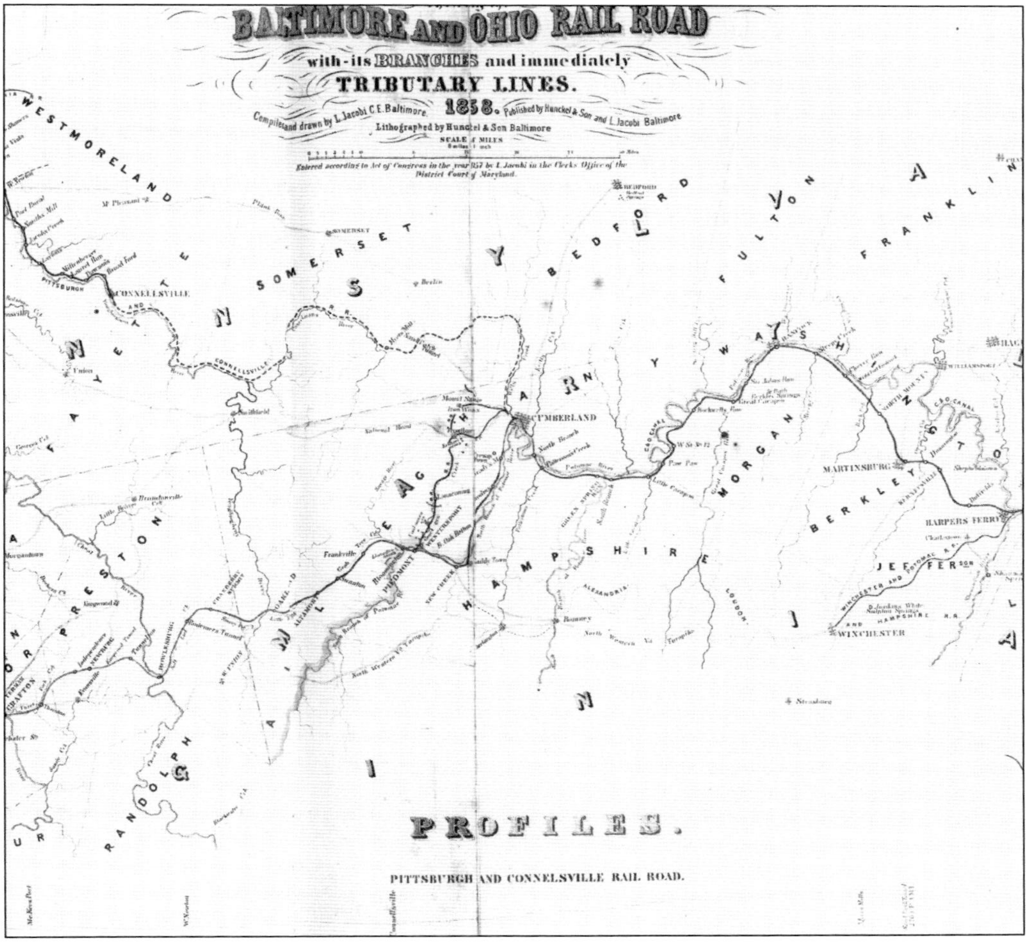

Bedford Springs was not the only spa resort in the Bedford area. The White Sulphur Springs Hotel, located in Milligan's Cove, near Mann's Choice, was constructed by Reed and Lyon from 1884 to 1887. The hotel was across from a sulphur spring known to area Native Americans and the valley's colonial settlers. This c. 1888 photograph shows the hotel building and gazebo over the sulphur spring. (Courtesy of Cliff Saxton Jr. and the White Sulphur Springs Museum and Archives.)

Because the spa resort was located in a very narrow valley and at a slight distance from Bedford, it was smaller in scale, with a more rural, rustic, and intimate atmosphere, as seen in this c. 1888 photograph. The two-story structure measured 100 feet in length and had 28 guest rooms. Also shown is the popular front porch, which wrapped around the hotel. (Courtesy of Cliff Saxton Jr. and the White Sulphur Springs Museum and Archives.)

In the 1890s, the hotel's new owners, the Colvin family, enlarged the building with a third story and added indoor plumbing, bathing facilities, and recreational buildings, such as a bowling alley. Wings were added to its rear, as shown in this c. 1930 photograph. (Courtesy of Cliff Saxton Jr. and the White Sulphur Springs Museum and Archives.)

This charming c. 1900 photograph, showing children playing in a tent set up at the White Sulphur Springs Hotel, emphasizes the resort's rural and relaxed atmosphere. (Courtesy of Cliff Saxton Jr. and White Sulphur Springs Museum and Archives.)

Among the outdoor activities available at the resort was croquet, as shown in this c. 1920 photograph of four women and a boy playing the game on the lawn. (Courtesy of Cliff Saxton Jr. and the White Sulphur Springs Historical Museum and Archives.)

This photograph shows the hotel as it appeared in 1888. Visitors came mostly from the central Pennsylvania and Cumberland, Maryland, areas, while other guests traveled from Philadelphia, Pittsburgh, Baltimore, Washington, DC, and New York City. Travel to the resort was by railroad lines of the Baltimore & Ohio Railroad from Cumberland, Maryland, and beyond as well as on the Bedford Division of the Pennsylvania Railroad. (Courtesy of Cliff Saxton Jr. and the White Sulphur Springs Museum and Archives.)

At first, travelers had to get off at Mann's Choice and travel by wagon to the hotel. A station was then built for the White Sulphur Springs Hotel, and visitors rode only a mile or so before arriving at the resort. (Courtesy of Cliff Saxton Jr. and the White Sulphur Springs Museum and Archives.)

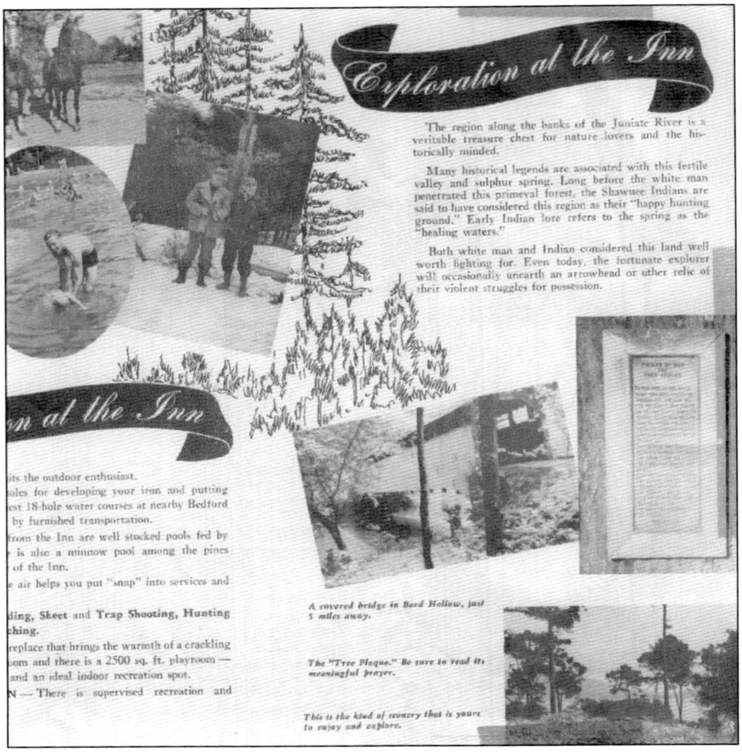

This is a c. 1950 brochure for the White Sulphur Springs Hotel. Guest registers of the early 20th century indicate that business at the White Sulphur Springs Hotel peaked between 1905 and 1915, then leveled off and remained constant until the mid-1930s. The increasing use of the automobile made the hotel more accessible. (Courtesy of Cliff Saxton Jr. and the White Sulphur Springs Museum and Archives.)

Colvin family members owned and operated the hotel from 1894 to 1946. By 1931, the White Sulphur Springs Hotel property contained 140 acres of mostly wooded land in the valley and on the surrounding mountains. Its rural quality was still emphasized in the hotel's brochure, as shown here. (Courtesy of Cliff Saxton Jr. and the White Sulphur Springs Museum and Archives.)

The White Sulphur Springs Hotel is notable for its intimate family atmosphere, which each of the owners managed to retain. In 1946, the property was sold to the Cochran family, who modernized the hotel, redecorated its interior, and added more outdoor amenities. After 32 years, the Cochrans sold the hotel to the Officers Christian Fellowship (OCF), which has retained the property since 1976 as a Christian retreat center for military officers and their families. Although it is no longer visited for its beneficial mineral springs, the hotel still draws many people, especially since the 2011 construction of its new hotel and conference facilities. The white sulphur spring and its gazebo, shown here in a c. 1888 photograph, remain on the property across the road from the original hotel building. (Courtesy of Cliff Saxton Jr. and the White Sulphur Springs Museum and Archives.)

Another springs resort in Pennsylvania that beckoned travelers was the Doubling Gap White Sulphur Springs Hotel in Newville, Cumberland County, Pennsylvania—not far from Bedford County. Native Americans used the mineral springs for centuries, followed by European settlers in the beginning of the 18th century. First established in 1803, the mineral springs resort was known by several names, including *Dublin Gap Sulphur Springs*, then *Doubling Gap White Sulphur Springs*, as shown on this advertisement. (Courtesy of Steve Long and the Doubling Gap Center.)

The first hotel building was constructed around 1803 and no longer exists. In 1846, the Doubling Gap Springs Association purchased the property. By 1848, a new owner had built a large stone hotel up the road from the original one. The hotel was enlarged when more buildings were added in the 1890s. This c. 1930 photograph shows the hotel's expansive wraparound porch, a must-have for resort hotels. (Courtesy of Steve Long and the Doubling Gap Center.)

In 1894, George A. Freyer of Philadelphia purchased the hotel, and it continued to prosper. Prominent Philadelphia-area people visited, including John Wanamaker and the DuPont family. Travelers arrived via the Pennsylvania Railroad to Harrisburg and then the Cumberland Valley Railroad to Newville, where a stagecoach met the train. This c. 1900 photograph shows the lobby with fashionable Victorian-era decor. (Courtesy of Steve Long and the Doubling Gap Center.)

One popular feature at the Doubling Gap White Sulphur Springs Hotel was a hike through the woods to the top of the mountain to a scenic lookout over the Cumberland Valley. The lookout was an outcropping known as Flat Rock, which still lures hikers today. This c. 1895 advertisement highlights Flat Rock and the resort's other features, such as the gazebo and Lake Henriette. (Courtesy of Steve Long and the Doubling Gap Center.)

THE SOCIAL CHARM OF

DOUBLING GAP

WHITE SULPHUR SPRINGS HOTEL

is due to the desirable class of its guests. The full complement of young men and women who summer there testify to the fact that Doubling Gap Springs Hotel has distinct social advantages. Doubling Gap White Sulphur Springs is unique among resorts. It is a retreat for those seeking health and at the same time a Social Mecca for those who go away for pleasure.

The tendency of the present-day medical advice is to the effect that all persons in selecting a place to spend their vacation time, should go, if possible, to a different climate and different environment from that of their usual life.

MEDICINAL SPRINGS

White Sulphur, Lithia, Iron, Magnesia

Dry, Cool, Bracing Atmosphere, Pine Groves, Mountain Brook, Boating, Bathing, Athletic and Children's Play Grounds, Tennis, Croquet, Golf, Garage and Boarding Stables, Riding and Driving, New Sanitary Plumbing, Suites and Rooms with Baths, Resident Physician.

Distances
225 Miles from New York City
135 Miles from Philadelphia, Pa.
280 Miles from Pittsburg, Pa.
158 Miles from Washington, D. C.
125 Miles from Baltimore, Md.

New Solarium, Delightful Piazza, with Lake View, Social Diversions, Billiards, Pool, Shuffle Boards, Large, Cheerful Dining Room, Our Own Milk, Vegetables, Poultry and Meats, Guests' Buffet Orchestra, Refined Entertainments, Automobile and Livery service to and from Hotel.

Bungalow Sites For Sale

Under Management of Owner
GEORGE ALBERT FREYER

DOUBLING GAP WHITE SULPHUR SPRINGS HOTEL

VIA. NEWVILLE

CUMBERLAND COUNTY, PENNA.

ALL INQUIRIES WILL BE ANSWERED PROMPTLY

A 1910 brochure claims that the Doubling Gap White Sulphur Springs Hotel has "distinct social advantages." Besides being a health retreat, it is called a "Social Mecca for those who go away for pleasure." The hotel had a solarium, a cheerful dining room, billiards, pool, shuffleboards, refined entertainment—with an orchestra, and automobile livery service to and from the hotel. (Courtesy of Steve Long and the Doubling Gap Center.)

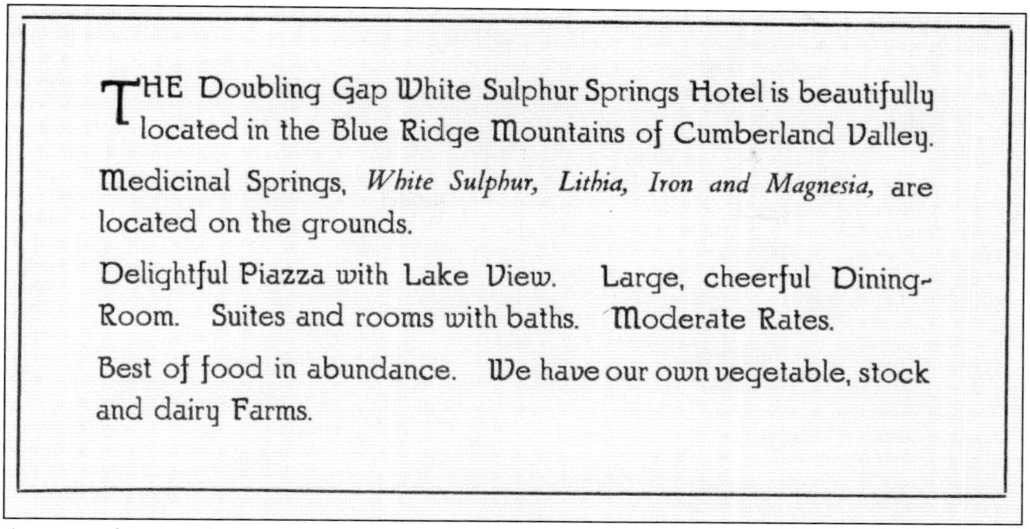
THE Doubling Gap White Sulphur Springs Hotel is beautifully located in the Blue Ridge Mountains of Cumberland Valley.

Medicinal Springs, *White Sulphur, Lithia, Iron and Magnesia,* are located on the grounds.

Delightful Piazza with Lake View. Large, cheerful Dining-Room. Suites and rooms with baths. Moderate Rates.

Best of food in abundance. We have our own vegetable, stock and dairy Farms.

A unique feature of the hotel was that it owned and operated its own farm, as mentioned in this c. 1920 booklet. A large barn housed livestock and dairy cows for meat, milk, cream, and butter for the hotel guests. The hotel also grew vegetables in an 11-acre garden, and a 25-acre orchard provided fruit for the guests. (Courtesy of Steve Long and the Doubling Gap Center.)

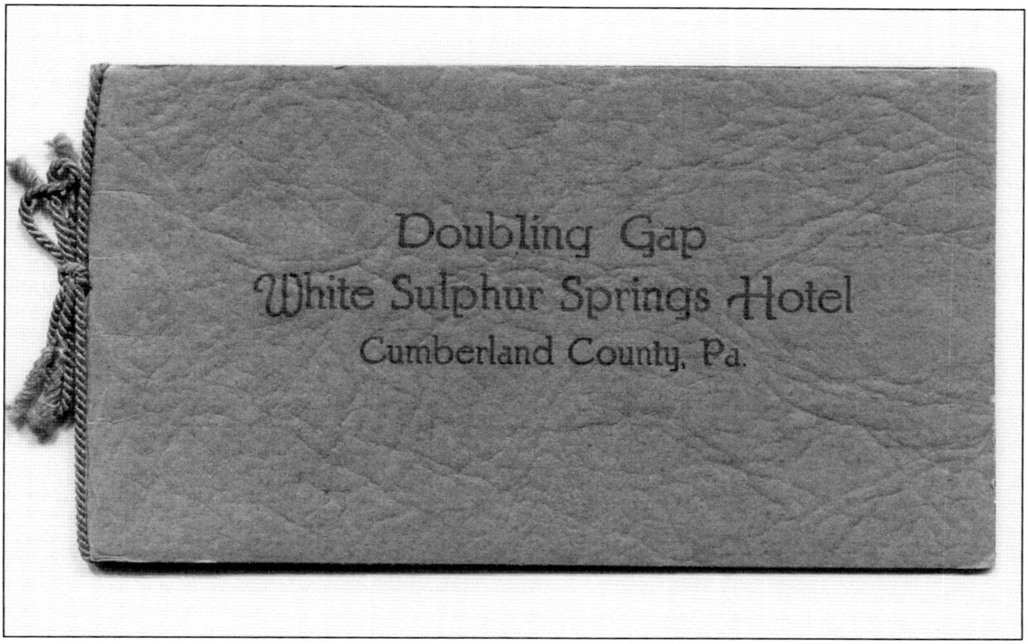

A c. 1920 booklet describes the medicinal springs on-site at the resort, including white sulphur, lithia, iron, and magnesia springs. Other main features of the resort were its "delightful piazza" (or porch) with a view of the lake, as well as suites and rooms with baths in them. (Courtesy of Steve Long and the Doubling Gap Center.)

The Doubling Gap White Sulphur Springs Hotel, like the Bedford Springs Hotel and other springs resorts, highlighted its spring by installing a decorative wooden gazebo over it, as shown in this illustration. (Courtesy of Steve Long and the Doubling Gap Center.)

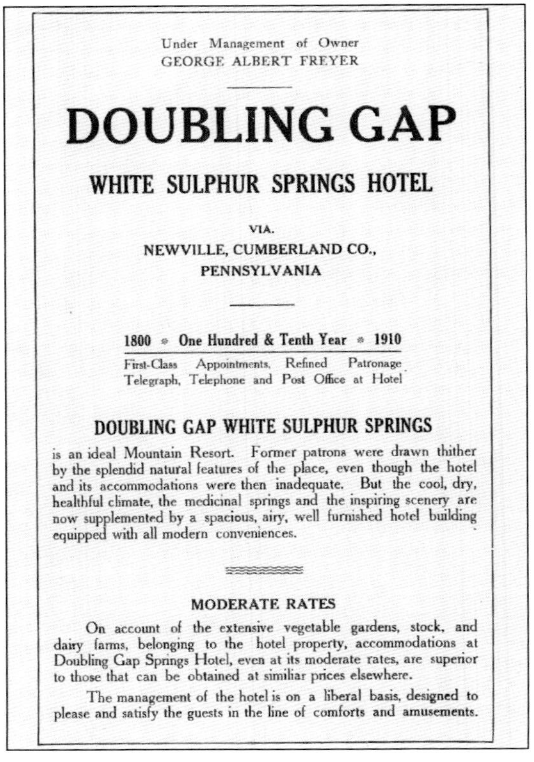

Under Management of Owner
GEORGE ALBERT FREYER

DOUBLING GAP

WHITE SULPHUR SPRINGS HOTEL

VIA.
NEWVILLE, CUMBERLAND CO.,
PENNSYLVANIA

1800 • One Hundred & Tenth Year • 1910

First-Class Appointments, Refined Patronage
Telegraph, Telephone and Post Office at Hotel

DOUBLING GAP WHITE SULPHUR SPRINGS

is an ideal Mountain Resort. Former patrons were drawn thither by the splendid natural features of the place, even though the hotel and its accommodations were then inadequate. But the cool, dry, healthful climate, the medicinal springs and the inspiring scenery are now supplemented by a spacious, airy, well furnished hotel building equipped with all modern conveniences.

MODERATE RATES

On account of the extensive vegetable gardens, stock, and dairy farms, belonging to the hotel property, accommodations at Doubling Gap Springs Hotel, even at its moderate rates, are superior to those that can be obtained at similiar prices elsewhere.

The management of the hotel is on a liberal basis, designed to please and satisfy the guests in the line of comforts and amusements.

In the early 20th century, the hotel struggled financially despite its advertisements, such as this c. 1925 brochure, and the efforts of a string of owners to keep it open. Unfortunately, the hotel was forced to close in 1935. In 1946, the East Pennsylvania Eldership of the Churches of God purchased the hotel property for its summer camp, Camp YoliJwa (standing for Youth Living Jesus' Way). (Courtesy of Steve Long and the Doubling Gap Center.)

Now known as the Doubling Gap Center, the facility continues to house Camp YoliJwa each summer. It also serves as a thriving conference and retreat center for many different organizations that come to enjoy its beauty and peacefulness. (Courtesy of Steve Long and the Doubling Gap Center.)

DOUBLING GAP
WHITE SULPHUR SPRINGS
HOTEL COMPANY
INCORPORATED

DOUBLING GAP
CUMBERLAND COUNTY
PENNSYLVANIA

Another page from the c. 1925 brochure is shown here. Lake Henrietta, whose name was changed from Lake Henriette, still has boating and fishing activities for campers and guests. (Courtesy of Steve Long and the Doubling Gap Center.)

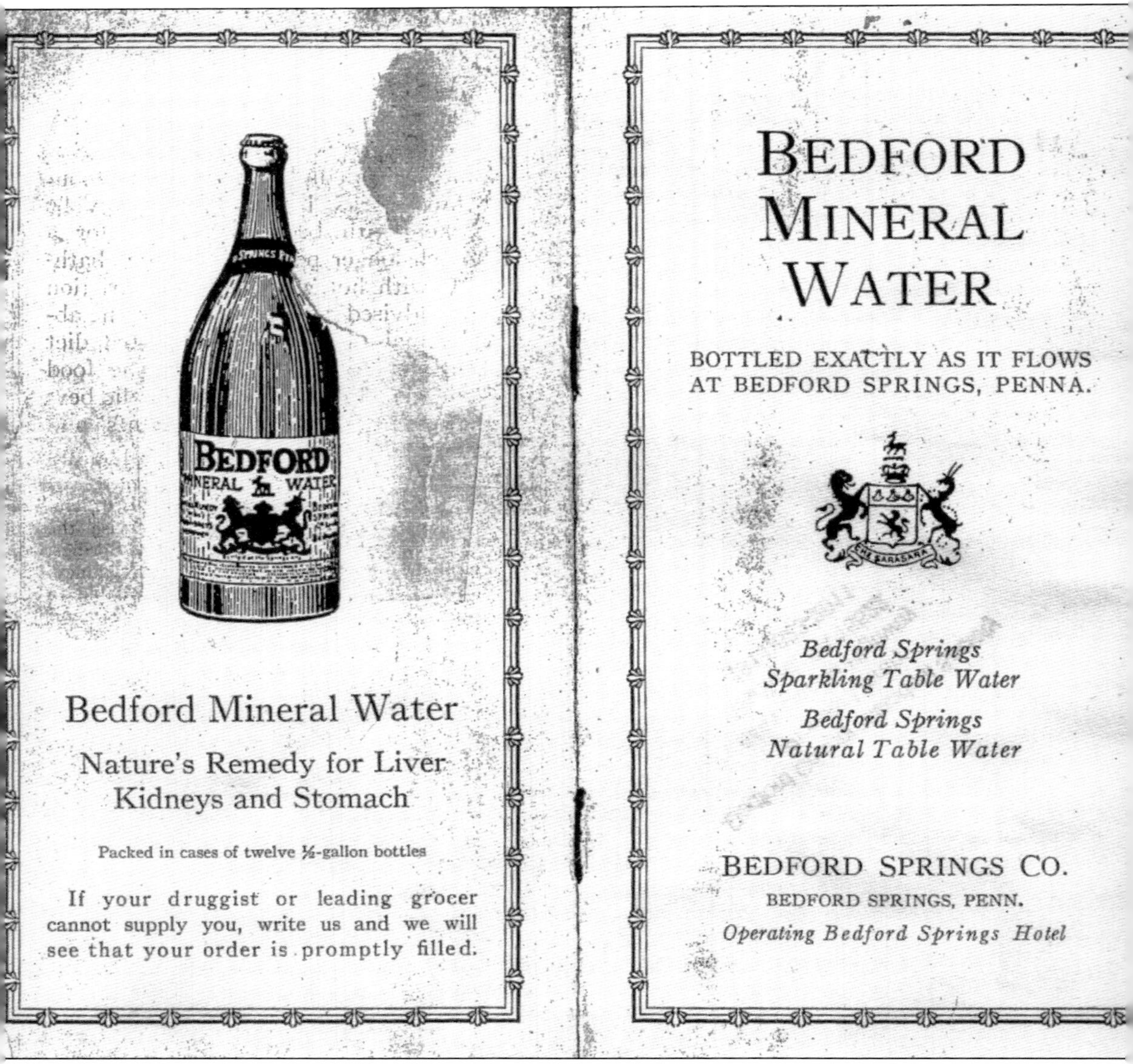

Mineral springwater became a popular product in the 1850s. The Bedford Mineral Springs Association was incorporated in March 1855 and started selling springwater in large quantities. Water was sold by the barrel for $3.25, by the half-barrel for $2.25, by the keg for $1.25, and by the glass carboy for $1.50. After using their barrels of water, customers purchased refills and had them shipped. In 1851, a scientist named Hector Humphreys from Annapolis, Maryland, analyzed the Bedford water's acidity and mineral content. In his letter to Espy Anderson, he concludes that the water is beneficial for bathing and washing and that its ingredients act favorably on the skin. He also states, "The action of the Bedford Water on my case (constipation of the bowels) was highly beneficial. I ought to have stayed at the Spring for a longer period." (Courtesy of the Bedford County Historical Society.)

This is a brochure advertising Bedford Mineral Water. By the 1880s, barrels of water were offered in different woods. Customers could order a "Galvanized, Iron-hooped barrel" of either mulberry or oak. Mulberry was a strong wood that did not dry out and was supposed to preserve the water for years, if necessary. Bedford Mineral Water was bottled in the mill building, which had been enlarged to become the "Bottling Plant."

After the arrival of the Pennsylvania Railroad near Bedford in 1854, Bedford Mineral Water was shipped to customers via railroad, as shown in this shipping order. Customers ordered water from towns and cities throughout Pennsylvania and the mid-Atlantic region.

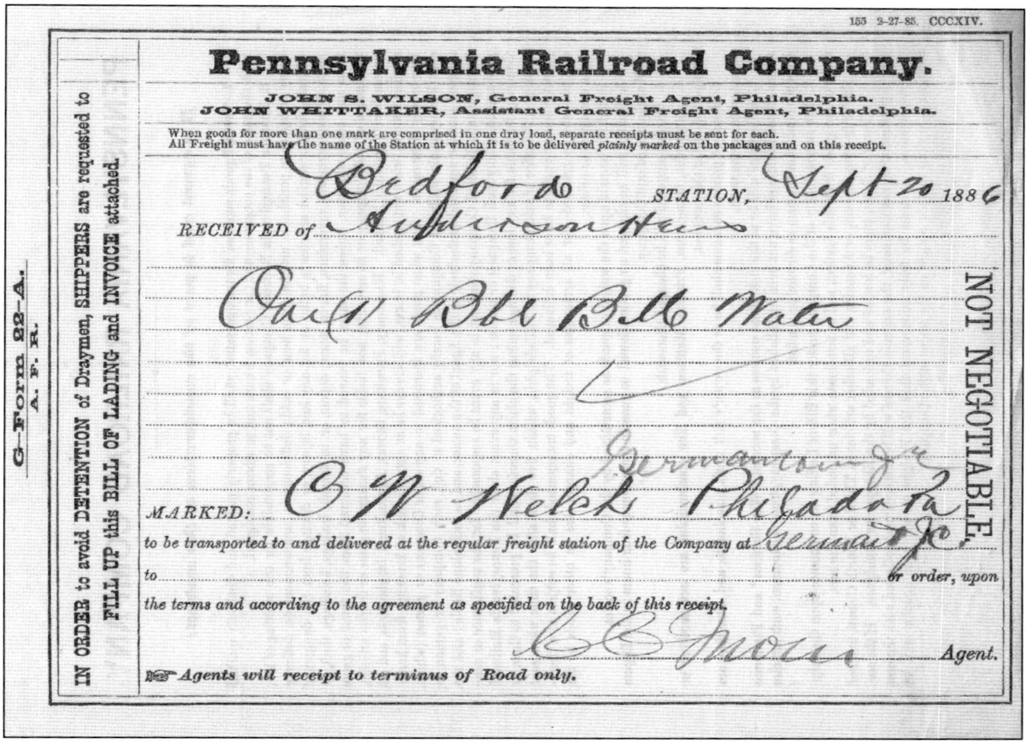

155 2-27-85. CCCXIV.

Pennsylvania Railroad Company.

JOHN S. WILSON, General Freight Agent, Philadelphia.
JOHN WHITTAKER, Assistant General Freight Agent, Philadelphia.

When goods for more than one mark are comprised in one dray load, separate receipts must be sent for each.
All Freight must have the name of the Station at which it is to be delivered *plainly marked* on the packages and on this receipt.

Bedford *STATION,* Sept 20 1886

RECEIVED of

MARKED:

to be transported to and delivered at the regular freight station of the Company at

to ... *or order, upon the terms and according to the agreement as specified on the back of this receipt.*

Agent.

Agents will receipt to terminus of Road only.

G-Form 22-A. A. F. R.

IN ORDER to avoid DETENTION of Draymen, SHIPPERS are requested to FILL UP this BILL OF LADING and INVOICE attached.

NOT NEGOTIABLE.

From the 1860s, doctors practicing the science of hydrotherapy published books on the mineral spa resorts in the country. In 1860, Dr. Sebastian Fonda published the mineral analysis of the magnesium springwater at Bedford Springs. The water contained mostly "sulfates of magnesium, followed by sulfate of lime, muriates of soda and lime, carbonates of lime and iron, and carbonic acid." The patrons in this 1861 photograph seem intent on having their water. The adults appear as though they have just arrived from the city, descended from the stagecoach, and gone directly

over to the magnesia spring. While the genteel group poses under the gazebo with glasses of water in hand, a hotel staffer (a "free man") and a young boy remain by the tree, ready to attend the guests. Walking sticks against the tree are waiting for visitors (but probably not this group) to use on their hikes on the mountain paths. Young people—perhaps the couples' children—are watching from the pavilion. Interestingly, the man with the wooden leg appears in another photograph of the hotel.

By the mid-19th century, the elite and the educated frequented the Bedford Springs Hotel. A number of US presidents visited the hotel throughout its history, including Pres. James Buchanan. A native and resident of Pennsylvania, Buchanan started visiting the mineral springs in 1816. This photograph of Buchanan was printed from a daguerreotype created by Mathew Brady between 1860 and 1870. (Courtesy of the Library of Congress.)

Buchanan spent a portion of his summers at Bedford throughout much of his adult life. After being elected president, he continued going to the resort, and in 1855, he spent the summer there, making it the Summer White House. This image was delineated by Nathaniel Currier in approximately 1856 from a photograph by Brady and then printed by Currier & Ives. (Courtesy of the Library of Congress.)

While at the Summer White House, President Buchanan received the first telegraph message over the newly laid Atlantic cable. Since 1842, repeated attempts had been made to lay submarine cable between North America and England. From 1857 to 1858, the crews of the USS *Niagara* and the HMS *Agamemnon* worked to lay the cable before finally succeeding. This commemorative print, created in 1866 after the cable had to be laid again, depicts the Atlantic cable as the "Eighth Wonder of the World." (Courtesy of Atlantic-Cable.com website.)

Finally, in August 1858, the endeavor was completed. Nationwide celebrations were topped by a communication from Queen Victoria to President Buchanan. Her message acknowledged American genius and English enterprise and celebrated the union of the Old and New Worlds. One can only imagine the celebration at the hotel once Buchanan received the communication from the queen. The certificate shown here commemorates the historic event. (Courtesy of Atlantic-Cable.com website.)

Mary Todd Lincoln, President Lincoln's widow, visited Bedford Springs in August 1868, according to the August 13, 1868, *Cambria Freeman*. She spent most of the summer with friends at the nearby Cresson Springs Hotel before a fall trip to Europe. Apparently, Mrs. Lincoln liked mineral baths and visited spring resorts in New York and the well-known spas in Baden Baden, Germany; Bath, England; and along the French Riviera. This photograph is from a carte de visite and was taken in 1872 by Mathew Brady. (Courtesy of the Library of Congress.)

Andrew Curtin, the governor of Pennsylvania from 1861–1867, reportedly visited Bedford Springs for tea on July 11, 1846. As one of Abraham Lincoln's biggest supporters, he was responsible for establishing the first and largest Civil War camp in Harrisburg, Pennsylvania, and was the first governor to send troops to defend Washington, DC. (Courtesy of the Library of Congress.)

Simon Cameron, a US senator from Pennsylvania and President Lincoln's first secretary of war, stayed at the Bedford Springs Hotel in the summer of 1872 along with other Republican politicians. This photograph of Cameron was taken between 1860 and 1870. (Courtesy of the Library of Congress.)

This intriguing photograph was taken in approximately 1885 and depicts a group, perhaps an extended family, relaxing on the front porch. The older gentlemen appear to be wistfully gazing out on the hotel's front lawn to the right of the photograph, perhaps reminiscing of earlier times at the hotel, while several of the group's younger people stare quite boldly at the camera lens. The porch was a busy place where many others congregated as well.

Three

Enjoying the Social Scene

The Bedford Springs Hotel was extremely successful between 1890 and 1930, and the resort provided a lively social scene for its visitors, as illustrated in this August 1891 photograph. Two important features were the resort's porch, which extended the length of the building (over 500 feet), and the front lawn, where many of the hotel's social interactions occurred. From left to right are Arthur Dougherty, Charlie Goldsborough, Isabel Boarman, ? Sherrerd, ? Howard, Nellie Sherrerd, Eliza Haldeman, Ashton Lurte, ? Weiner, and Casper Drill.

In 1890, the Anderson House was constructed north of the Swiss Building. Watson Diehl, who built the White Sulphur Springs Hotel in Milligan's Cove (mentioned earlier), matched the architecture of the other structures. The porches across all of the buildings were altered to harmonize with each other. This c. 1890 photograph shows the row of structures from the Colonial Building at the left to the Anderson House on the far right.

Five years earlier, in 1885, the Crockford Building had been removed from the hotel's front lawn and relocated to a place south of the Colonial Building, opening up the front lawn for more activity. This postcard shows another c. 1890 view of the Anderson House, with the open lawn barely visible on the left of the photograph.

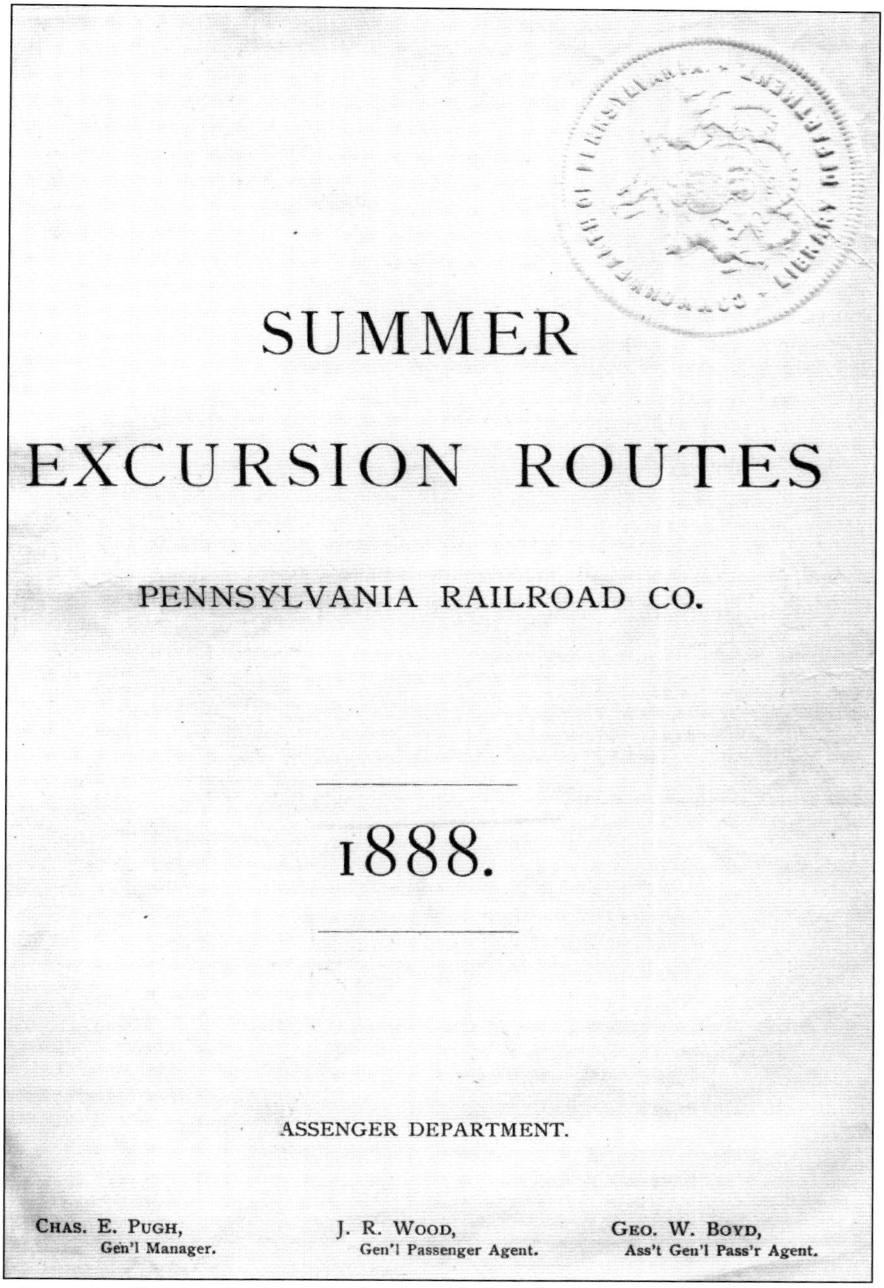
SUMMER

EXCURSION ROUTES

PENNSYLVANIA RAILROAD CO.

1888.

ASSENGER DEPARTMENT.

Chas. E. Pugh,	J. R. Wood,	Geo. W. Boyd,
Gen'l Manager.	Gen'l Passenger Agent.	Ass't Gen'l Pass'r Agent.

Summer Excursion Routes was an annual book published from the 1870s through the early 1890s by the Pennsylvania Railroad Company's passenger department. It lists all the destinations that the Pennsylvania Railroad system offered as well as schedule and ticket information. This image depicts the title page of the 1888 travel guide. Purchasers of an excursion fare had all the privileges of a first-class ticket holder. It seems that, just like today, there were some restrictions when purchasing a ticket: round-trip tickets sold from June 1 to September 30 had to be used by October 31; children between 5 and 12 paid half fare; and those over 12 paid full fare. Baggage up to 150 pounds was checked for free, and anything heavier was charged.

Summer Excursion Routes includes flowery descriptions and illustrations of beautiful scenery available to sojourners by traveling the Pennsylvania Railroad. Travelers could visit Niagara Falls, the Adirondacks, and the Catskills in the north or travel to Warm Springs, Virginia, or the New Jersey seashore. To appeal to more than one class of traveler, the excursion guide advertised a range of Bedford hotels, including the Arandale Hotel (capacity 200), Bedford House (capacity 60), Chalybeate Hotel (capacity 150), Corel House (capacity 50), East End Cottages (capacity 100), Hotel Arlington (capacity 50), Hotel Waverly (capacity 100), Union House (capacity 50), and the Washington House (capacity 75). Topping the list was the Bedford Springs Hotel, with a capacity of 700. This illustration is from the 1880 edition of the *Summer Excursion Route* guidebook. (Courtesy of the Pennsylvania State Library.)

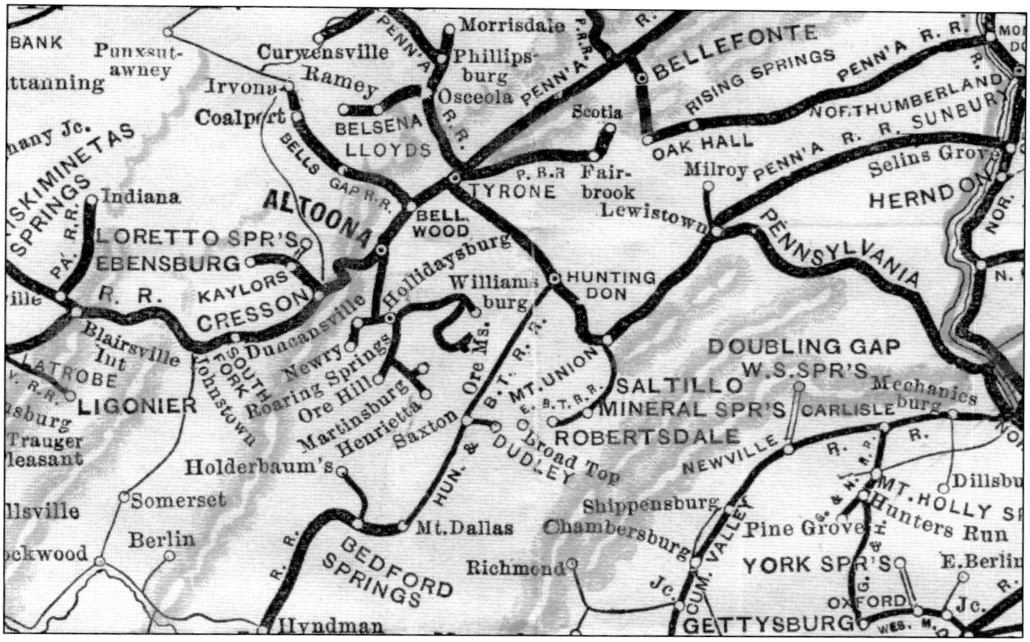

This close-up of the 1880 railroad map shows the Bedford stop (called Bedford Springs) on the Bedford Division of the Pennsylvania Railroad. The map is included in the 1880 edition of the railroad's *Summer Excursion Routes*. (Courtesy of the Pennsylvania State Library.)

PENNSYLVANIA RAILROAD.—Branches Continued. 139

BEDFORD DIVISION.

Wm. H. Brown, Superintendent, Bedford, Pa.

STATIONS.	Mls	Accom.	Mail.
Lve. **Huntingdon** 1			8 00 A.M.
" **Mt. Dallas** 2	0		11 15 "
" Ashcom	2		11 21 "
" Lutzville	3		11 26 "
" Jameson	5		11 33 "
" **Bedford**	8	7 30 A.M.	11 50 A.M.
" Wolfsburg	11	7 42 "	12 02 NO'N
" Napier	13	7 50 "	12 10 P.M.
" Mann's Choice	16	8 03 "	12 23 "
" Sulphur Springs	18	8 11 "	12 31 "
" Buffalo Mills	21	8 23 "	12 42 "
" Londonderry	22	8 29 "	12 48 "
" Preston	27	8 48 "	1 06 "
" Wills Creek	30	9 00 "	1 18 "
" **Bridgeport** 3	31	9 03 "	1 21 "
" Cook's Mill	36	.. ..	.. ..
" State Line	39	.. ..	.. ..
Arr. **Cumberland** 4	45	9 55 A.M.	2 08 P.M.

STATIONS.	Mls	Mail.	Accom.
Lve. **Cumberland** 4	0	9 35 A.M.	5 10 P.M.
" State Line	6	.. ..	.. ..
" Cook's Mill	9	.. ..	.. ..
" **Bridgeport** 3	14	10 25 "	6 00 "
" Wills Creek	15	10 28 "	6 03 "
" Preston	18	10 39 "	6 15 "
" Londonderry	23	10 56 "	6 33 "
" Buffalo Mills	24	11 02 "	6 39 "
" Sulphur Springs	27	11 13 "	6 50 "
" Mann's Choice	29	11 20 "	6 58 "
" Napier	32	11 31 "	7 11 "
" Wolfsburg	34	11 39 "	7 19 "
" **Bedford**	37	11 55 A.M.	7 30 P.M.
" Jameson	40	12 02 NO'N	
" Lutzville	42	12 09 P.M.	
" Ashcom	44	12 14 "	
" **Mt. Dallas** 2	45	12 25 "	
Arr. **Huntingdon** 1		3 20 P.M.	

CONNECTIONS.

1 With Main Line Pennsylvania Railroad.

2 With Huntingdon and Broad Top Railroad.

3 With Pittsburg, Washington and Baltimore Railroad.

4 With Baltimore and Ohio Railroad.

CONNECTIONS OF PENNSYLVANIA RAILROAD AND BRANCHES.

1 With all railroads diverging from Philadelphia, north, south, and east.
2 Junction of West Chester and Philadelphia Railroad with Main Line.
3 Junction of Waynesburg Branch with Main Line.
4 Junction of Wilmington and Reading Railroad with Main Line.
5 Junction of eastern end of Columbia Branch with Main Line.
6 Reading and Columbia Railroad crosses Main Line.
7 Junction of western end of Columbia Branch with Main Line.
8 With Cumberland Valley, and Lebanon Valley Railroads, and Northern Central Railway.
9 Junction of Dauphin and Susquehanna Railroad with Main Line.
10 Northern Central Railway crosses Main Line.
11 Junction of Mifflin and Centre County Branch with Main Line.
12 Junction of Huntingdon and Broad Top Railroad with Main Line.
13 Junction of Bald Eagle Valley and Clearfield Divisions with Main Line.
18 With railroads diverging from Pittsburg.
19 With York Branch, and with Reading and Columbia Railroad.
20 Chester Valley Railroad intersects with Waynesburg Branch.
21 Junction of Bellefonte and Snow Shoe Railroad with Bald Eagle and Clearfield Divisions.
22 Junction of Philadelphia and Erie Railway.
23 Junction of Bald Eagle and Clearfield Divisions.
24 Junction of Western Pennsylvania Division with Indiana Branch.
25 Junction of Allegheny Valley Railroad with Western Pennsylvania Division.
26 Junction of Butler Extension with Western Pennsylvania Division.
27 Junction of Sunbury and Lewistown Railroad with Mifflin and Centre County Branch.
28 Junction of Lewistown Division with Northern Central Railway.

The consolidated Bedford Division includes the short lines of the Huntingdon & Broad Top Mountain Railroad, as well as the Bedford and Bridgeport Railroad, and extended from Huntingdon, Pennsylvania, to Cumberland, Maryland, as shown on this Bedford Division timetable. According to *Summer Excursion Routes*, Excursions 5, 6, 21, 24, and 1222 stopped at Bedford. (Courtesy of Cliff Saxton Jr. and the White Sulphur Springs Historical Society.)

In the early 1890s, a local lensman took many photographs of the hotel guests in various places on the property, many of which are shown in this chapter. Dates are handwritten at the bottom of many of the images, and some have people's names written on them (which are not shown here). A favorite spot for the guests to sit for photographs was the front porch. The young people in this July 1892 image are, from left to right, Sue Dalzell, Alice Sellers, Frank Jones, Spencer Gilbert, Mrs. Gilbert, James Park, and Mrs. Park.

The front lawn was another place where hotel guests congregated, as shown in this c. 1890 photograph that includes Baltimore resident Isabel Boarman and three unidentified gentlemen. The hotel attracted notable people in the 1890s, including J. Pierpont Morgan of the New York banking house Drexel, Morgan & Company. During one week in July 1891, both Pennsylvania governor Robert Pattison and Maryland governor Elihu Jackson visited the hotel.

The windows of the Colonial Building were a popular setting for group photographs, as shown in this July 1896 image. An interesting person in this and many of the photographs is a Mr. Olmsted, visible inside the window frame in the back row. Olmsted was a Harrisburg attorney who reportedly was a chaperone for the hotel's young guests, accompanying them in many of their activities for several years in the early 1890s.

Another group poses in the window of the Colonial Building in this July 1896 photograph. Unfortunately, no one is identified.

The couple in this c. 1890 photograph appears to be in the middle of a conversation.

Shown here in a group photograph on the porch in July 1892 are, from left to right, (first row) Spencer Gilbert, Mrs. Gilbert, and James Park; (second row) Mrs. Park, Frank Jones, Sue Daltzell, and Alice Sellers.

Different kinds of parties were held on the front porch. This July 1895 photograph shows three women having a "lemonade party," as the photograph's handwritten caption indicates. They are, from left to right, Carrie Hillis, May Latrobe, and Mary ?.

In August 1892, a group poses during a "cake party" on the porch. Mr. Olmsted is at the left, with, from left to right, ? Haldeman, Annie Simonton, Ashton Lurte, and Eliza Haldeman.

BILLIARD and Pool Tables, Bowling Alleys, Tennis Courts and Golf Links.

The Sanitary arrangements are all modern and safe. The Service good. The Culinary Department is under the immediate attention and supervision of the Manager.

The Lawn is lighted with Electric (Arc) Lights and the Porches with Gas, making the whole scene at night very brilliant and cheerful.

In 1899, the hotel issued a small brochure in the form of a pocket-sized booklet, which was similar to the one shown previously for the Doubling Gap White Sulphur Springs Hotel. The brochure describes the activities available at the resort and also assures prospective visitors that the hotel is sanitary—a special concern to travelers, in light of recent epidemics, such as the yellow fever epidemic in 1898 and smallpox and diphtheria epidemics in 1899.

THE

BEDFORD SPRINGS

HOTEL AND BATHS

OPEN JUNE TO OCTOBER
H. E. BEMIS, H. M. WING
Managers
NEW YORK OFFICE, 243 FIFTH AVENUE
WINTER
HOTEL ROYAL POINCIANA, PALM BEACH, H. E. BEMIS, *Manager*
FLORIDA EAST COAST HOTEL COMPANY

By 1899, a management partnership called the Florida East Coast Hotel Company, operated by H.E. Bemus and H.M. Wise, managed the Bedford Springs Hotel. In the winter, Bemus also operated the Hotel Royal Poinciana in Palm Beach, Florida, according to this brochure.

Bicycle riding was one of the outdoor activities offered at the Bedford Springs Hotel. This group of three women has paused for a photograph in approximately 1892 with two of their male friends. Bicycle Willow parties were held, in which groups traveled to the Willows (formerly Defibaugh's Tavern) for their bicycle ride. The bicycles were most likely transported with the group in a wagon over to the Willows.

Shober's Run provided its own entertainment as groups of friends ventured across very narrow, wooden-plank bridges and posed for photographs, as seen in this July 1895 image. This bridge appears to have been located south of the main bridge that crossed the creek to the Magnesia Pavilion.

Looking at the group in this July 1895 photograph, one wonders if anyone ever slipped off the bridge and into the creek. While now a person would photograph the entire hilarious scene, it was probably frowned upon to do so at the time.

This July 1895 photograph shows a group of fun-loving friends out for a walk on Constitution Hill. They have posed on a bench with their backs toward the photographer.

One can almost hear the giggling and joking as this group waits for the photographer to snap the photograph. Mr. Olmsted appears at the far right of the group.

The hotel was no doubt a place where "best friends forever" were made. These two girls are Julia Small from York, Pennsylvania, and Annie Simonton from Harrisburg, visiting the hotel in July 1892. This photograph appears to have been taken after the girls took off their hats, perhaps at the end of an active and fun afternoon.

White blouses with lacy, ruffled necklines and cinched waists were typical of women's fashion in the 1890s. Note Julia Small's brooch at her throat. It appears to be a portrait brooch and was possibly painted on porcelain.

This c. 1892 photograph shows a hotel guest, Lois Bailey, spending some quiet moments in the garden of what appears to be the nearby log cabin. The log cabin remains north of the hotel property to this day.

Hats were a fashion staple in the 1890s and ranged anywhere from straw boater's hats to those adorned with ribbons and flowers. During this decade, hats were worn squarely on top of the head over an upswept hairdo. Imagine the fun (and maybe anxiety) these ladies may have had while ordering their just-right hats from the milliner and their custom-fit dresses from their dressmakers in time for their departure for Bedford Springs.

Germans were regular social events at Bedford Springs. The name referred to a dance party in the Pennsylvania area and came from the name of the prominent dance traditionally held at such events, the german cotillion. The dance was derived from the French patterned dance known as the cotillion, meaning "petticoat." Adults sponsored germans at Bedford Springs, including a Mrs. Graham, who sponsored this one in August 1895.

While most germans were held at night, apparently some took place in the daytime. A Mrs. Robinson hosted one in the morning in July 1895. This photograph appears to have been taken in front of the Evitt Building.

This german appears to have had a theme. The c. 1890 photograph depicts many of the young ladies holding flowers or wearing them in their hair, and some of the young men are wearing sashes. The group is posing at the sulphur spring gazebo.

A Miss Weiss also sponsored a morning german in July 1895, according to a caption on this photograph. The large group poses at the sulphur springs gazebo. It appears that germans were popular at the resort and kept the young people busy. Without a doubt, the dances enabled young men and women to meet each other, perhaps inviting the start of promising new friendships.

"Tally Ho" parties used the hotel's stagecoach to take visitors on excursions to local places around the countryside. Parties were organized, and many crowded into the stagecoach for the ride. Other wagons joined the group for the excursions as well, as illustrated in this

1894 photograph. It appears that Sen. Stephen B. Elkins from West Virginia is standing second from left in the row of people in front of the carriages.

In this c. 1892 photograph, Mr. Olmsted (left) is reading to the others while they relax around the table.

A group on the porch is making party favors for a german, perhaps for Mrs. Robinson's or Miss Weiss's morning german in July 1895. From left to right are Mr. Olmsted, May Latrobe, May Colket, Don Haldeman, and Carrie Hillis. Note the mask that Olmsted is holding.

This is another page from the 1898 brochure with its elegant graphics. The booklet advertises the resort's amenities, management, and the dates of the summer season, from June 27 to October 3.

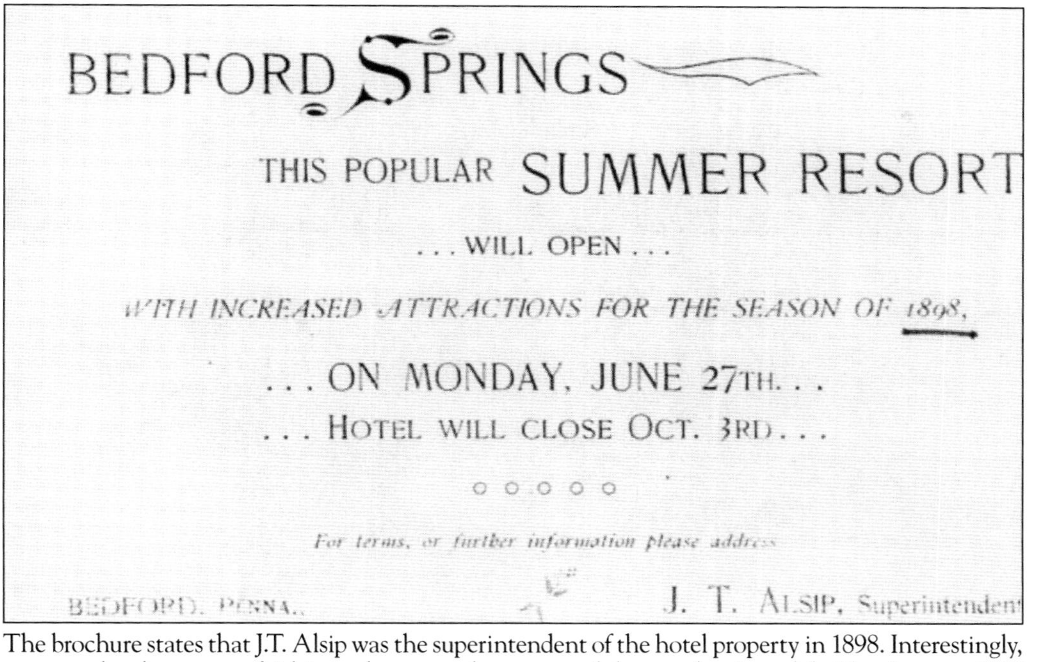

The brochure states that J.T. Alsip was the superintendent of the hotel property in 1898. Interestingly, a person by the name of Alsip is shown as the owner of the nearby Arandale Hotel on an 1898 map of the area, which is shown on page 10.

Card games were another pastime at the resort. The group in this undated photograph is playing whist, a popular game in the 18th and 19th centuries. Whist was derived from the older game of ruff and honours. For much of the 20th century, bridge replaced whist as the most popular card game among serious card players. In this photograph are, from left to right, Fred Nichols, ? Nelson, Isabel Boarman, and Sally Fisher.

The group in this August 1892 photograph is playing six-handed euchre on the porch of the Colonial Building. Euchre may have been introduced to the United States by early German settlers who called the game *Juckerspiel*, and it is responsible for introducing the joker into modern decks of cards. From left to right are Ruth Bailey, R. Barbour, Eddie Richardson, Mr. Olmsted, Isabel Boarman, Captain Barbour, and Regina Barbour.

This group is playing a card game on the front lawn during what appears to be a hot day in July 1896. From left to right are Billy Wallace, ? McCormick, unidentified, Steve Elkins Jr., unidentified, Julia Small, unidentified, Mary ?, unidentified, Don Haldeman, and ? Pitcairn.

Although details of the people in this July 1896 photograph are indistinct, the photograph is notable for its iconic and dramatic shapes that are representative of the photograph's era—the lady's ornate hat, the sun-shading parasol, and the gentlemen's hats—all set against the balustrade and turned columns of the hotel building.

A Miss Martine hosted a "Tally Ho" party in July 1894. Posing in her finery and surrounded by friends (including Mr. Olmsted), Miss Martine may have been celebrating her birthday.

This is a photograph of the entire group and its carriages during Miss Martine's party in July 1894. The party may have been en route to dinner at the Willows, which was previously known as Defibaugh's Tavern.

Another entourage is dressed to go to the Willows in the "Tally Ho" stagecoach. Just a pleasant 20-minute ride from the resort, the Willows provided an enjoyable destination for resort guests during their stay. No visit to Bedford was considered complete without a visit to the Willows for its famous chicken dinner. The establishment was known for its Chicken à la Maryland, a broiled chicken dinner using a proprietary recipe.

The bandstand was a popular place for guests to congregate and pose for the camera. The wooden structure was constructed in front of the Evitt Building in 1880 and painted contrasting colors to match the hotel and the other wooden features on the lawn. This photograph was taken around 1892.

The chambermaids and their managers posed for this group photograph on the front lawn in 1903. Hotel employees included many local Bedford residents as well as those who came from surrounding towns. Many current Bedford families have ties to the Bedford Springs Hotel through relatives who worked there. Poses are relaxed in this photograph, and the camaraderie and friendship among the girls are evident.

In this August 1893 photograph are Melnie Hatch and Ashton Lurte, who may have later married, as evidenced by a caption on a later photograph that identifies a woman with her baby as "Mother Lurte." When young women became engaged at the hotel, they carved their signatures in the window glass with their diamonds. The glass panes with the signatures have been retained and are still evident in different windows on the hotel's first floor.

Dogs in the 1890s were no different than dogs of today. This well-dressed gentleman probably got very wet a minute after the photograph was taken when the wet dog shook himself out after playing in the creek. Both are standing on the other side of Shober's Run, possibly in the vicinity of the crystal spring, another mineral spring on the property.

The rocks of Federal Hill were another scenic spot where people posed for group photographs, as seen in this c. 1890 image. A man in the rear left pretends to be reading to the others, while Captain Barbour in the front left holds back a smile. Isabel Boarman is in the rear, and Mr. Olmsted is at the far right. The names of the others are unknown.

Another group poses for the camera against the Federal Hill rocks. Ashton Lurte and Melnie Hatch are in the center of the front row, and the others are unidentified.

In this July 1895 photograph, James Milliken is sitting on the porch railing and leaning against the column, while Mr. Olmsted sits on the floor and reads a newspaper to him and Miss DeValesco.

This August 1895 photograph shows, from left to right, (first row) Stephen B. Elkins Jr. and Bessie Baccus; (second row) Miss DeValesco, James Milliken, and Sen. Stephen B. Elkins, from West Virginia.

Miss DeValesco and James Milliken pose for a photograph against the rocks of Federal Hill in this July 1895 photograph.

Older guests also posed in group photographs. This distinguished-looking group has gone for a stroll and is posing with a dog in front of the rocks of Federal Hill. The dog appears to be the same dog by the creek in a previous photograph.

The wooden turnstile at the sulphur spring was a favorite place for the young people to gather and pose, as seen in this c. 1892 photograph.

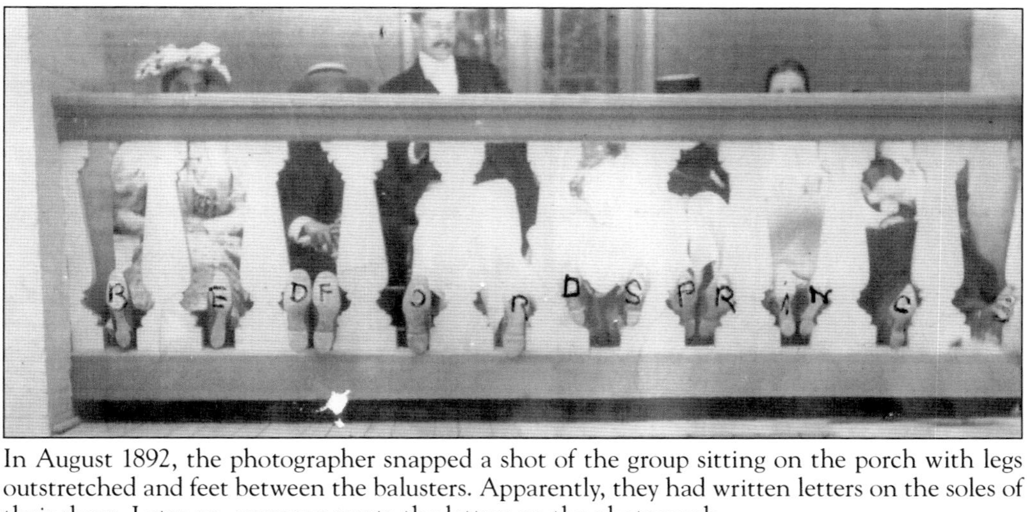

In August 1892, the photographer snapped a shot of the group sitting on the porch with legs outstretched and feet between the balusters. Apparently, they had written letters on the soles of their shoes. Later on, someone wrote the letters on the photograph.

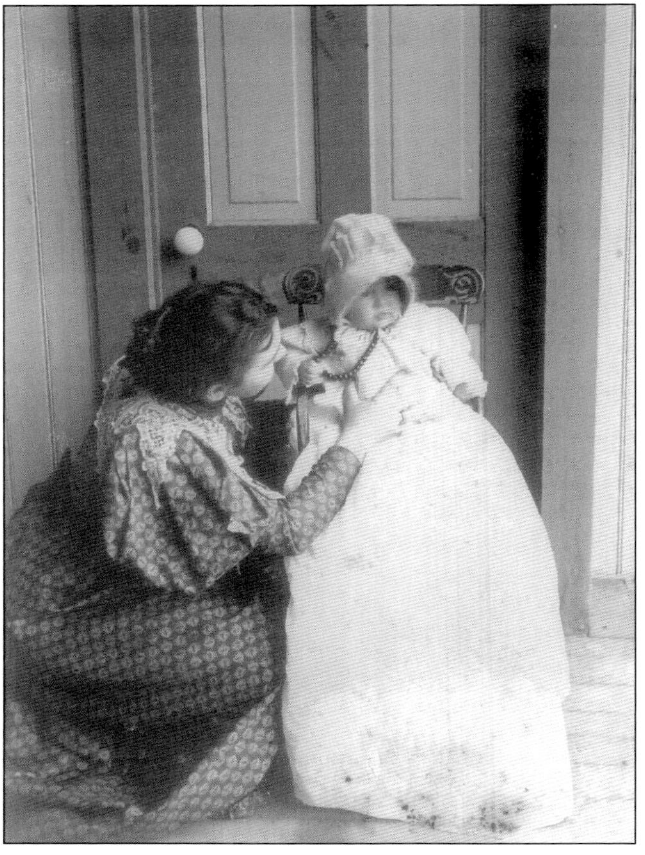

The Bedford Springs Hotel was a family resort, and mothers brought their babies and children. It was not uncommon for families to stay at the resort for several weeks or months at a time, while the fathers stayed in the city working. This July 1895 photograph shows baby "Jimmy" and his mother, whose last name appears to be "Lurte" in a photograph caption, which gives further evidence that Melnie Hatch and Ashton Lurte may have gotten married.

Children were not photographed as frequently as adults, probably because they could not sit still long enough to pose for the camera. The photographer caught this child (whose name is illegible on the photograph) as he sits alone on the porch playing. He is wearing a popular outfit of the day—a sailor's suit. The photograph is undated.

Baby Jimmy and his mother pose with their dog, Charlie, against the rocks of Federal Hill in this July 1895 photograph.

Picnics were another favorite activity at the Bedford Springs Hotel, and people liked to walk up the mountain to the fire tower behind the hotel and picnic on the lawn at the tower's base or elsewhere on the hotel grounds. In this undated photograph, a group of women and girls is picnicking among the rocks.

This undated photograph shows another fun-loving group of unidentified people posing for the camera, this time from behind a hedge.

This July 1895 photograph shows a group sitting on the porch of the Colonial Building. Second from the left is Luis Hartranft, followed by, from left to right, ? Ethel ?, Minnie Bosler, Mr. Olmsted, Andrew Reeder, Isabel Boarman, and Dan Drill. The woman in the window and the gentleman beside her are unidentified.

Another group includes, from left to right, Steve Elkins Jr., Mr. Olmsted, May Latrobe, Dan Drill, Mary ?, Don Haldeman, Carrie Hillis, and Joe ?, who line up in front of the fence for a funny group shot.

A group of young people poses for a photograph in front of a coach in this July 1896 photograph. From left to right are Dick McGraw, Patti Rodgers, Davis Elkins, unidentified, John Davis, and the unidentified driver, who is seen several times in these images.

A series of comical photographs was taken in August 1892, when the group demonstrated three different emotions for the photographer, as indicated in the handwritten caption. Hilarity is shown in this photograph. Compare this August 1892 image with those taken in the 1860s, when it was de rigueur to project formality and a somber demeanor. What a difference!

Surprise is shown in this photograph. From left to right are Captain Barbour, Regina Barbour, Mr. Olmsted, unidentified, Ollie Richardson, Isabel Boarman, and unidentified. Most of those identified have already appeared in previous photographs.

The same group as above projects Anger for the camera.

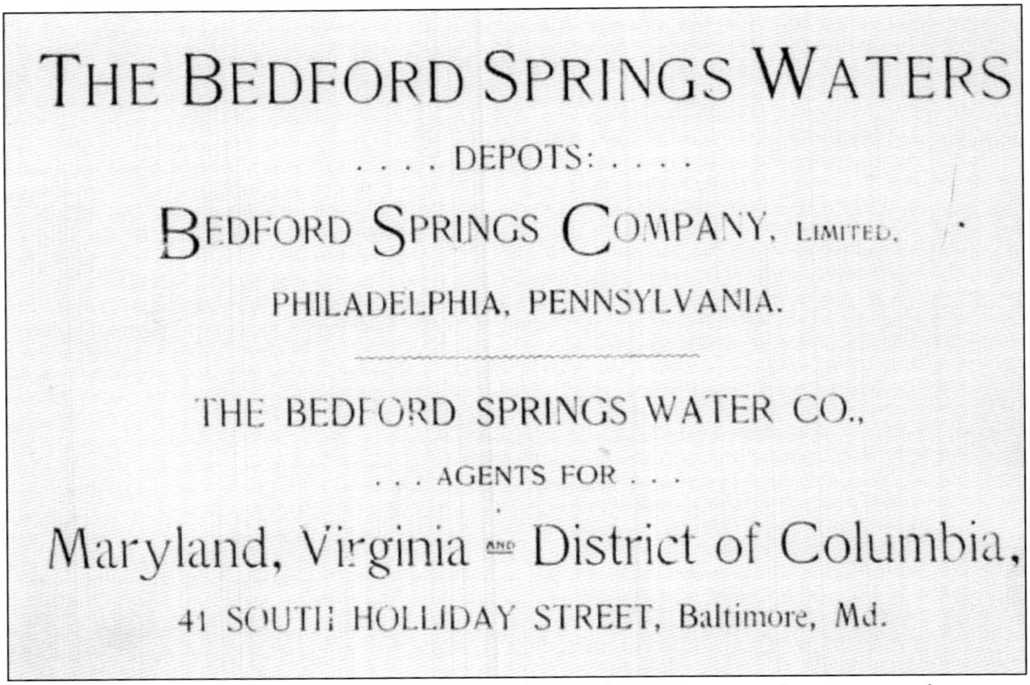
THE BEDFORD SPRINGS WATERS

. . . . DEPOTS: . . . .

BEDFORD SPRINGS COMPANY, LIMITED.

PHILADELPHIA, PENNSYLVANIA.

THE BEDFORD SPRINGS WATER CO.,

. . . AGENTS FOR . . .

Maryland, Virginia AND District of Columbia,

41 SOUTH HOLLIDAY STREET, Baltimore, Md.

More pages from the 1899 brochure are shown here. This page is an advertisement for agents selling the Bedford Springs Water out of their Philadelphia and Baltimore locations. The Baltimore agent sold the water to customers in Maryland, Virginia, and Washington, DC.

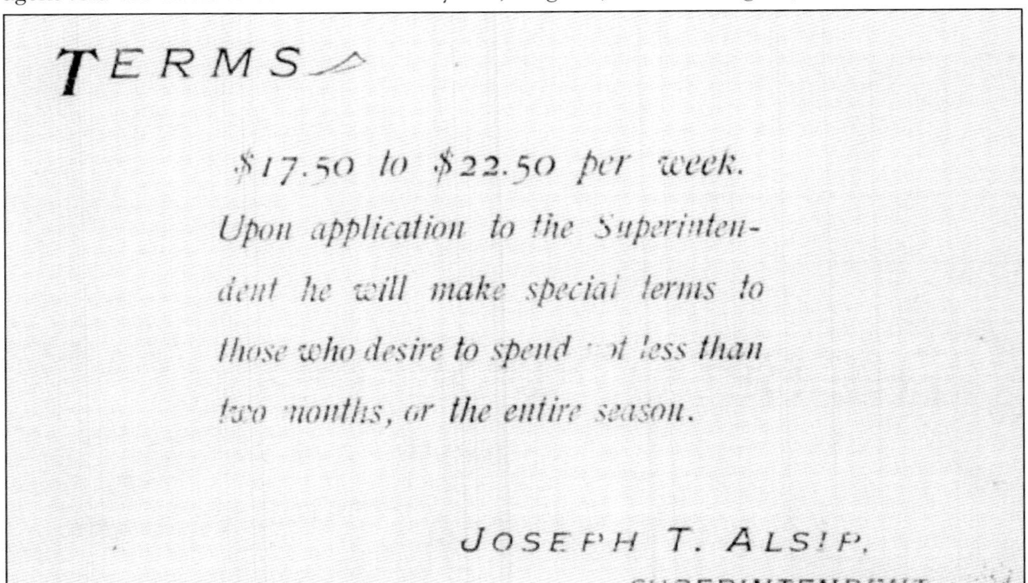
TERMS

$17.50 to $22.50 per week.

Upon application to the Superintendent he will make special terms to those who desire to spend not less than two months, or the entire season.

JOSEPH T. ALSIP,

SUPERINTENDENT.

According to this 1899 brochure, the rates for a week's stay at the hotel during the 1899 summer season ranged from $17.50 to $22.50 per week. Longer stays of several months or the entire season were, of course, available as well.

This group poses against a stone masonry wall and staircase on Constitution Hill.

Another jovial group poses for a photograph against the rocks on Constitution Hill. The young men in the front row are unidentified. In the back row, from left to right, are Lois Bailey, Frank ?, Bessie Baccus, Steve Elkins Jr., Patti Rodgers, Frank Eshleheim, Ruth Bailey, Mary Eshle[heim], unidentified, Mary Laughlin, and Davis Elkins.

Girlfriends Emma Gildersleeve (left), ? Barrie (center), and Georgie Ford are setting out for a stroll on the front lawn of the hotel, which is seen in the background.

In this August 1894 photograph are, from left to right, Dan Drill, Laura Diller, unidentified, Leonie DeBarey, Melnie Hatch, Carrie Hiller, and Mr. Olmsted, with Ashton Lurte sitting in front.

This photograph shows, from left to right, Ashton Lurte, Leonie DeBarey, Melnie Hatch, and Mr. Olmsted.

A group poses in the yard of the Willows during this July 1896 Willow Bicycle Party. From left to right are (first row) unidentified, Eliza Haldeman, and Ruth Bailey; (second row) Don Haldeman, Toni Baldridge, Joe Bancroft, and Arthur Dickson. Carrie Hillis is in the back between the trees.

This is a c. 1892 close-up of the group posing at the wooden turnstile at the sulphur spring. Several have climbed on it and are striking dramatic poses.

The sulphur spring gazebo is shown in this postcard. It matched the other wooden features of the lawn and was constructed at the same time as the new wooden bridge, which led to the magnesia spring and pavilion. Bertha, the postcard's sender, exclaimed to her friend, "Catherine, this place is beautiful."

Three young men and two women pose for the camera on the front lawn in this August 1895 photograph. From left to right are Dan Drill, Bessie Baccus, Don Haldeman, Ruth Bailey, and Steve Elkins Jr.

Sitting in chairs and on the ground, the well-dressed group in this c. 1892 photograph might be listening to a concert on the front lawn or preparing to go to a Willow party.

The young men and women in this group pose on the lawn in this 1896 photograph. The Colonial Building can be seen in the background. From left to right are (first row) Eugene ?, Don Haldeman, Billy Hill, Steve Elkins Jr., Archie ?, and John ?; (second row) Billy Pearson, Davis Elkins, Madge Rutherford, Ruth Bailey, Carrie Hillis, Eliza Haldeman, May Latrobe, and Dan Drill.

Lying on the grass in a row in this August 1892 photograph are, from left to right, Mr. Olmsted, Vinnie Pattison, Captain Barbour, Regina Barbour, Ollie Richardson, Ruth Bailey, and Columbus ?.

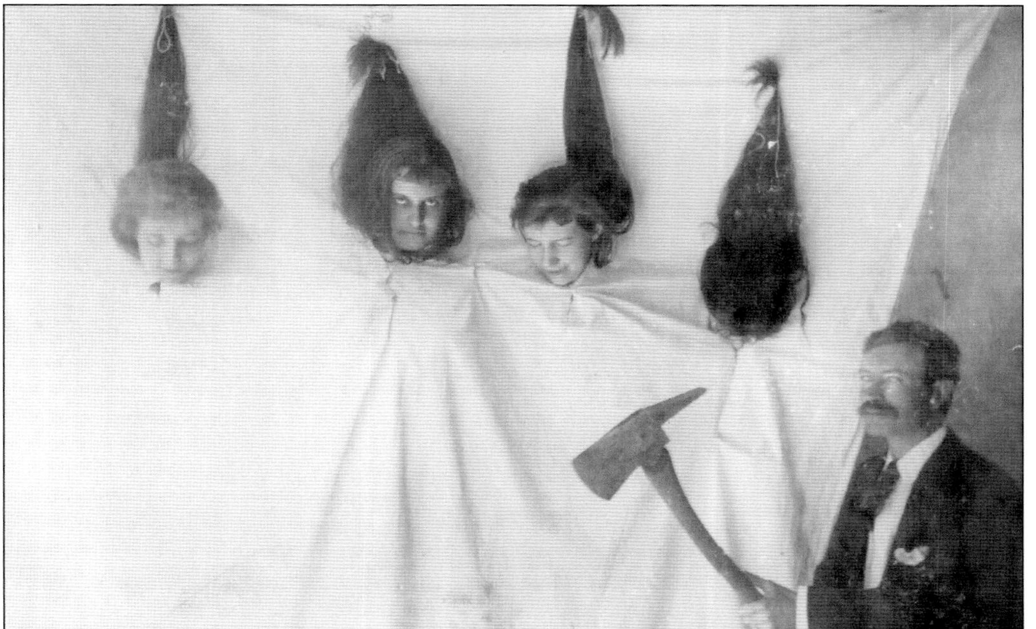

The hotel guests performed dramas, such as *Bluebeard the Pirate*. In this August 1892 photograph, the actors are, from left to right, Regina Barbour, Annie Simonton, Ruth Bailey, ? Barbour, and Mr. Olmsted, playing Bluebeard.

Although it was primarily a resort known for its social scene, the Bedford Springs Hotel was still advertised for its therapeutic waters at the turn of the century. In an 1899 article in the *American Monthly*, a travel column writer refers to the hotel as the "Carlsbad of America," comparing it with the German spa resort. "Why cross the Atlantic for sojourn at any of the European spas when there is an American Carlsbad almost at your door?" he asks. He states that the "Bedford Water" has no superior among known mineral waters for all functional diseases of the liver and digestive organs, and that the baths produced results in every way as satisfactory as those of the most famous of the German spas. He asks, "Why not take the 'Bedford Cure'?" Advertisements for the resort claimed that its therapies were endorsed by the best medical authorities in America.

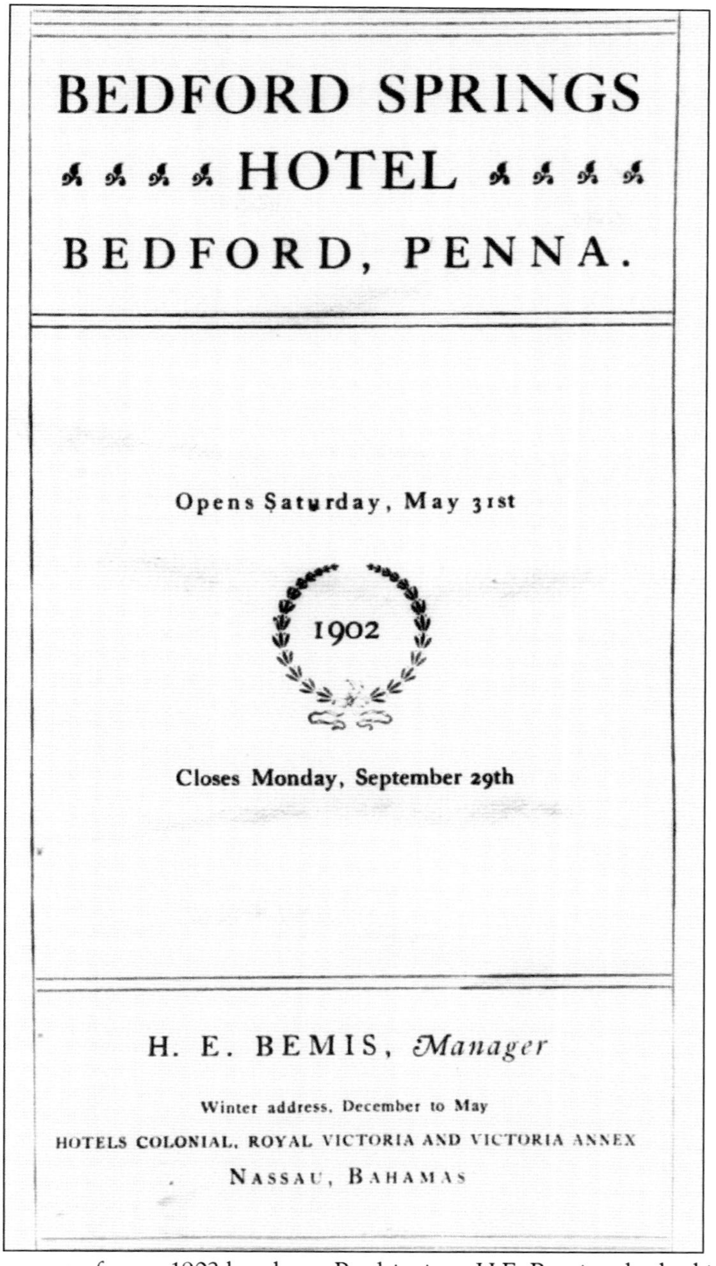
BEDFORD SPRINGS

HOTEL

BEDFORD, PENNA.

Opens Saturday, May 31st

1902

Closes Monday, September 29th

H. E. BEMIS, *Manager*

Winter address, December to May

HOTELS COLONIAL, ROYAL VICTORIA AND VICTORIA ANNEX

NASSAU, BAHAMAS

Both of these pages are from a 1902 brochure. By this time, H.E. Bemis, who had just come from upstate New York's Lake Mohonk Mountain House, was the manager of the hotel. According to the brochure, the Bedford Springs Hotel had an excellent orchestra and first-class cuisine, and the golf links were said to be unsurpassed by any in the state. Rooms for two people were $26 to $50 per week, with bathrooms connected to the rooms an extra $10.50 to $12 per week. Professional organizations started to hold their meetings and conferences at the hotel early on. In 1906, both the Medical Society of the State of Pennsylvania and the Pennsylvania State Bar Association held their annual meetings there. The Pennsylvania State Teachers' Association also convened at the hotel, as did the Pennsylvania Homeopathic Medical Society.

In the 1920s, a tennis court was installed on the southern end of the hotel's front lawn in front of the laundry building. A judge's stand was on one side of the court, and a viewing stand was next to it. This postcard shows a view of the tennis court with the judging stand to the right.

By 1912, annual tennis tournaments were held at the Bedford Springs Hotel. The viewing stand is toward the back in this postcard image.

This 1926 photograph shows an active game of tennis at the hotel, with the laundry building behind it.

Shober's Run and Constitution Hill form a beautiful backdrop for the tennis courts in this postcard view. One postcard message, dated 1915, reads, "Of course we could not think of staying anywhere else." Another one reads, ". . . will take one Bedford Springs Hotel—the other is an imitation."

Court golf, or lawn golf, was a precursor to miniature golf, and a court was located on the hotel's front lawn from 1890 to 1910. According to one brochure, it attracted many of the guests, "especially the ladies." This c. 1906 photograph depicts a front lawn filled with activity—between the game of court golf underway, its spectators, and the automobiles coming and going.

In court golf, players tried to hit the ball into nine holes that were arranged in a circle around a central turning ground. Obstacles, such as trees, mounds, and hedges, were used to challenge the players, as shown in this 1900 photograph taken during a lull in activity on a quiet summer afternoon.

Water was still ordered and shipped from the Bedford Springs Hotel Company, Ltd., as seen in this 1906 letter accompanying a shipment of water to a customer in Uniontown, Pennsylvania.

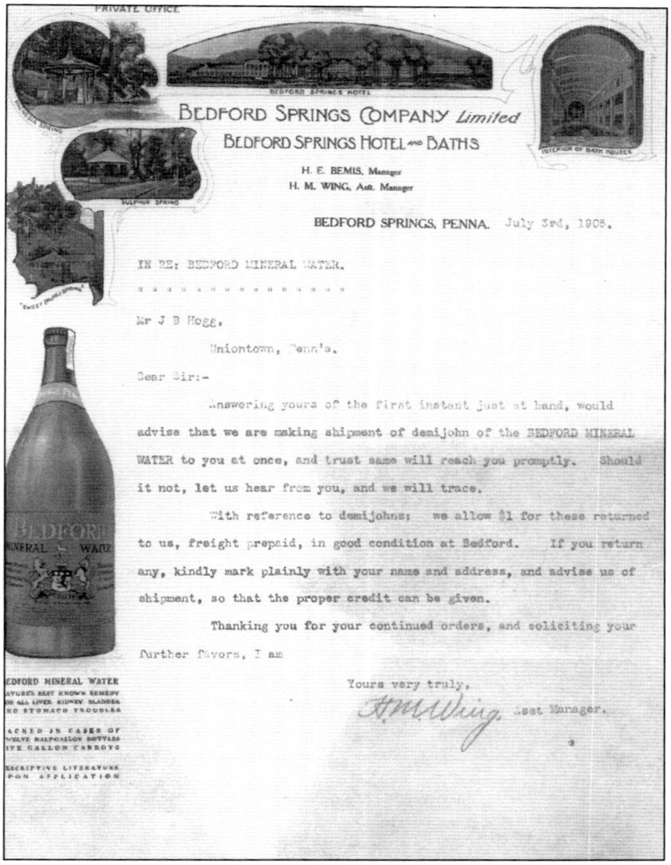

PRIVATE OFFICE

BEDFORD SPRINGS COMPANY *Limited*

BEDFORD SPRINGS HOTEL AND BATHS

H. E. BEMIS, Manager

H. M. WING, Ass't. Manager

BEDFORD SPRINGS, PENNA. July 3rd, 1905.

IN RE: BEDFORD MINERAL WATER.

Mr J B Hogg,

Uniontown, Penn'a.

Dear Sir:-

Answering yours of the first instant just at hand, would advise that we are making shipment of demijohn of the BEDFORD MINERAL WATER to you at once, and trust same will reach you promptly. Should it not, let us hear from you, and we will trace.

With reference to demijohns: we allow $1 for these returned to us, freight prepaid, in good condition at Bedford. If you return any, kindly mark plainly with your name and address, and advise us of shipment, so that the proper credit can be given.

Thanking you for your continued orders, and soliciting your further favors, I am

Yours very truly,

H. M. Wing, Asst Manager.

BEDFORD MINERAL WATER

This 1909 stationery is an example of a prewritten postcard that guests could send out with their travel information and next address. Many hotel guests spent their summers visiting a series of resorts, one after another, and these postcards kept friends and family apprised of their travels. Interestingly, postcards sold during this time were frequently printed in Germany and published by local merchants, such as Edward D. Heckenman, a druggist in town.

BEDFORD SPRINGS, N. Y. 1909

WE ARRIVED HERE AT .... M. TODAY. LEFT .... AT .... M. DISTANCE .... MILES. WEATHER .... ROADS ....

EXPECT TO LEAVE .... FOR ....

NEXT ADDRESS FOR MAIL WILL BE ....

In 1905, an indoor swimming pool (also called the Bath House) was constructed south of the Colonial Building between the laundry building and the tennis courts. Its architectural style blended well with the Colonial Building. This postcard depicts the new swimming pool and the laundry building behind it.

This postcard depicts a closer view of the new swimming pool, claimed by some to be the country's first indoor pool. The building featured a semicircular wraparound porch on the ground floor and a gallery surrounding the second story. Clerestory windows on three sides allowed plenty of sun into the pool.

In 1991, large-format photographs were taken of the vacant hotel buildings and grounds as part of a recordation for the Historic American Buildings Survey/Historic American Engineering Record (HABS/HAER), a program operated by the National Park Service. This photograph depicts a view of the vacant swimming pool building. The second-story railing on the southern end had been removed by then. (Courtesy of the Library of Congress.)

The interior of the swimming pool was lined with white tile, as seen in this c. 1905 postcard, and featured a dramatic, sweeping double stairway at one end (not shown here). Mineral spring water was piped into the swimming pool. Another postcard that someone sent from the hotel in 1909 reads, "Greetings from the well."

More improvements came in 1905, when a continuous colonnade was constructed on the front of the property. The dramatic two-story colonnade carried hotel guests from the front of the Colonial Building across the broad lawn and over to the bridge crossing Shober's Run. This c. 1905 photograph illustrates how the colonnade originated at the second story and extended over the front drive.

After crossing the front lawn, the colonnade connected to the grand staircase and bridge over Shober's Run, as shown by this postcard, which states, "This is a nice place for you to come this summer."

This postcard shows another view of the colonnade and its connection to the bridge over the road and creek to the right. Beyond the bridge is the magnesia spring pavilion. The 1880s bridge was removed in the 1960s and reconstructed.

This postcard shows a side elevation of the colonnade and a song that must have been played daily, the "Morning Call."

Morning concerts were played from the bandstand on the lawn, and guests sat under the colonnade, relaxing and enjoying the concert, as shown in this c. 1905 postcard.

The automobile age arrived at the Bedford Springs Hotel after the turn of the century, and guests increasingly drove to the resort. This 1914 photograph shows two unidentified couples in front of the Bedford Springs Hotel in what appears to be a new car.

The front lawn next to the tennis court was turned into a parking lot to accommodate all the cars, as seen in this c. 1905 postcard.

Automobiles are lined up on the road in front of the hotel for what appears to be a motorcade or procession in this c. 1905 postcard. A spring gazebo is in the background.

A lone car on the winding drive leading down to the Bedford Springs Hotel is shown in this c. 1905 postcard.

The road in front of the hotel was lined with a section of the stone wall on one side, which probably was the original 1850s wall, and a wooden post and rail fence on the other side next to Shober's Run, as shown in this c. 1910 postcard. Part of the stone wall has been retained and is visible at the front entrance today.

A renewed interest in hydrotherapy prompted Dr. William Edward Fitch to publish a book in 1927 called *Mineral Waters of the United States and American Spas*. His goal was to help the medical profession realize the importance of American mineral water resources and their therapeutic value in treating chronic diseases. He became the resident physician of the Bedford Springs Hotel and Baths, and between 1927 and 1929, he published a series of pamphlets, including *Chronic Arthritis*, *Chronic Diseases of the Liver*, *Obesity*, *Arteriosclerosis*, and *Sciatica*. The pamphlets recommended therapies, such as balneotherapy, crounotherapy, dietotherapy, and exercise. By the late 1920s, different baths and showers were available at the resort, including an "electric light cabinet bath," a "needle shower bath," a "rain shower bath," a "hot spout bath," and a "Nauheim bath." This postcard shows the magnesia springs pavilion and the limestone spring gazebo in the distance.

Four

Golfing the Links

The Bedford Springs Hotel's 169-acre golf course, one of the first 6,000-yard courses in the country, was constructed in 1895 by Spencer Oldham and redesigned by A.W. Tillinghast in 1912. In 1923, during the golden age of golf course design, famed golf course architect Donald Ross redesigned the course, making it, according to local historian and *Bedford Gazette* writer and editor Ned Frear, "one of the very best in Pennsylvania." This 1906 postcard depicts players and spectators on the original course, which is now the site of the 10th green.

LOCAL RULES

White stakes, roads and fences mark out of bounds. Penalty: Loss of distance.

A ball in or over ditches parallel to holes No. 1, 4, 9, 15, 17 and 18 is out of bounds.

The pond, creek, and streams are water hazards, drop on margin with loss of one stroke.

A ball driven from tee into stream or bank of stream on Nos. 3, 7, 9 and 11, may be lifted and dropped not nearer the hole, without penalty.

A ball lying on putting green other than green played to, must be lifted and dropped off the green not nearer the hole, without penalty.

Single players or matches exceeding four players have no right on the course.

If a match fails to maintain its place and loses more than one clear hole of players in front it may be passed upon request.

CADDIES are assigned by Caddie Master
Fees: 9 Holes, 75; 2 bags, $1.25
18 Holes, $1.25; 2 bags, $2.00

Replace Cut Turf

Tee BETWEEN markers, not in front.

BEDFORD SPRINGS
Hotel & Golf Club

BEDFORD, PENNSYLVANIA

SCORE CARD

U. S. G. A. Rules govern all play unless modified by local rules on back page.

Contrary to popular belief, it appears that Spencer Oldham's original 6,000-yard course had 18 holes. The course featured a geometric S-curve and donut bunkers that still exist. When Tillinghast redesigned the course in 1912, he made nine longer holes from the 18 original ones that Oldham had constructed. Tillinghast added a par-three hole, a favorite that he nicknamed "Tiny Tim." This scorecard (also below) is from the 1950s.

BEDFORD SPRINGS GOLF CLUB

PAR (MEN'S)	4	3	5	3	5	4	4	4	4	36	3	4	4	5	3	4	5	3	4	35	71		
DISTANCE YARDS	318	193	497	197	505	316	365	303	445	3139	113	435	396	573	93	398	564	165	326	3063	6202		
HOLES	1	2	3	4	5	6	7	8	9	OUT	10	11	12	13	14	15	16	17	18	IN	TOT.	HANDICAP	NET SCORE
MATCHES WE																							
WON + LOST — HALVED O HANDICAP STROKES	13	11	5	3	7	15	9	17	1		16	6	10	4	18	8	2	14	12				
THEY																							
WOMEN'S PAR	4	3	5	3	5	4	4	4	5	37	3	5	5	5	3	5	5	3	4	38	75		

←THIS CARD SIX INCHES WIDE→

*SCORER*__________

*DATE*__________ *ATTEST*__________

When Donald Ross redesigned the course in 1923, he kept six of the holes and added 12 more. According to Ned Frear, its showpiece was hole No. 4, a difficult shot requiring a long wood shot to an elevated green, with steep slopes, trees, and deep traps.

The redesigned golf course was highly acclaimed. After the 1923 reconstruction, the *Pittsburgh Post* reported, "Pittsburgh golfers who have played over the Bedford Springs Course are loud in their praise of the newly constructed links near the big summer hotel." It also claimed that the course added to the attractiveness of the town as a vacation center. This c. 1925 postcard depicts men and women on the golf course.

In the background of this c. 1925 photograph is the nine-story Barclay House, constructed in 1923 on the hill behind the other hotel buildings. After the Barclay House and Donald Ross golf course were constructed, the resort's owner, Delaware businessman Samuel Bancroft, planned on constructing another building next to the Barclay House that would overlook the golf course. The building was never constructed. The clubhouse shown here on the right was built in 1923.

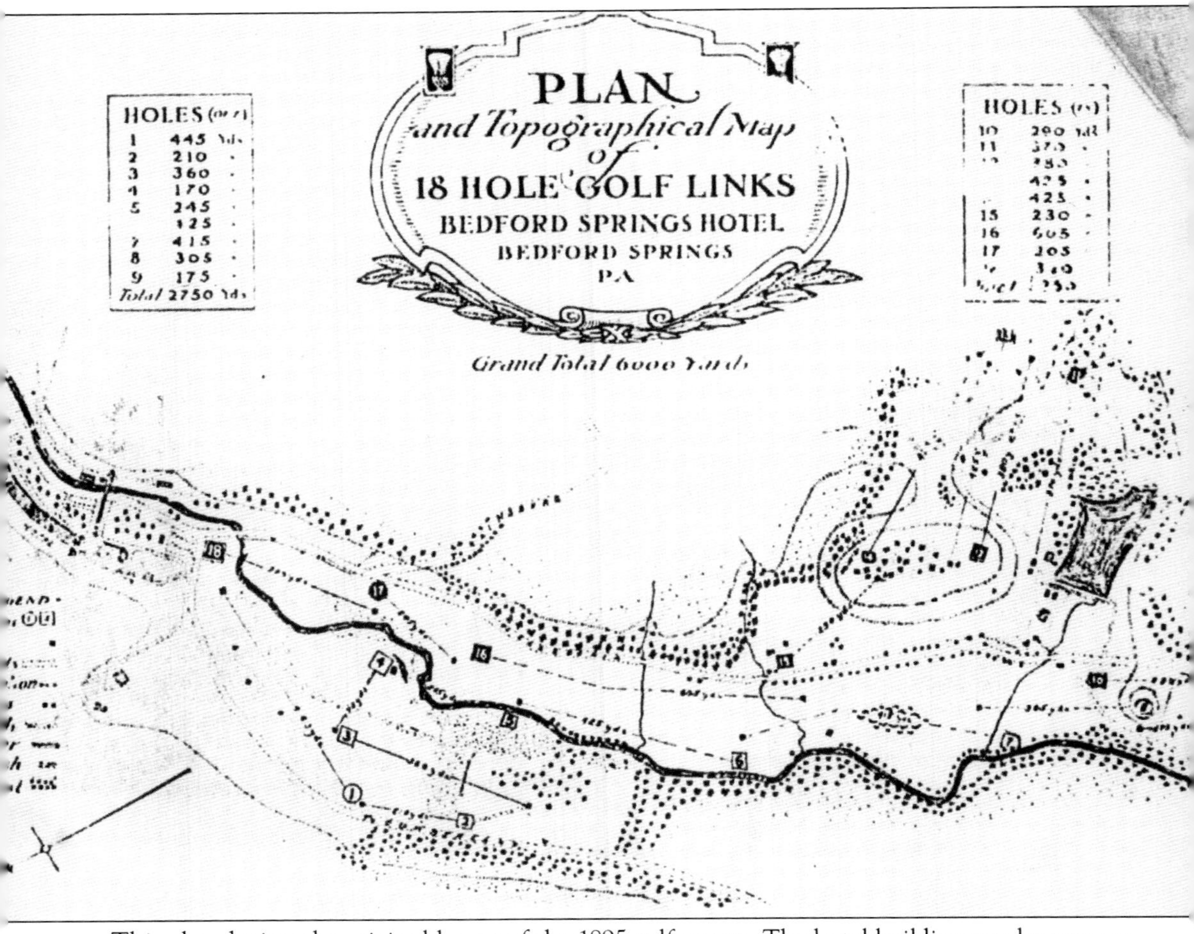

This plan depicts the original layout of the 1895 golf course. The hotel building can be seen on the left, with Shober's Run meandering through the property. Holes one through five are on the northwestern side of the creek, and the remaining holes are on the southern side, with the 18th hole closest to the hotel.

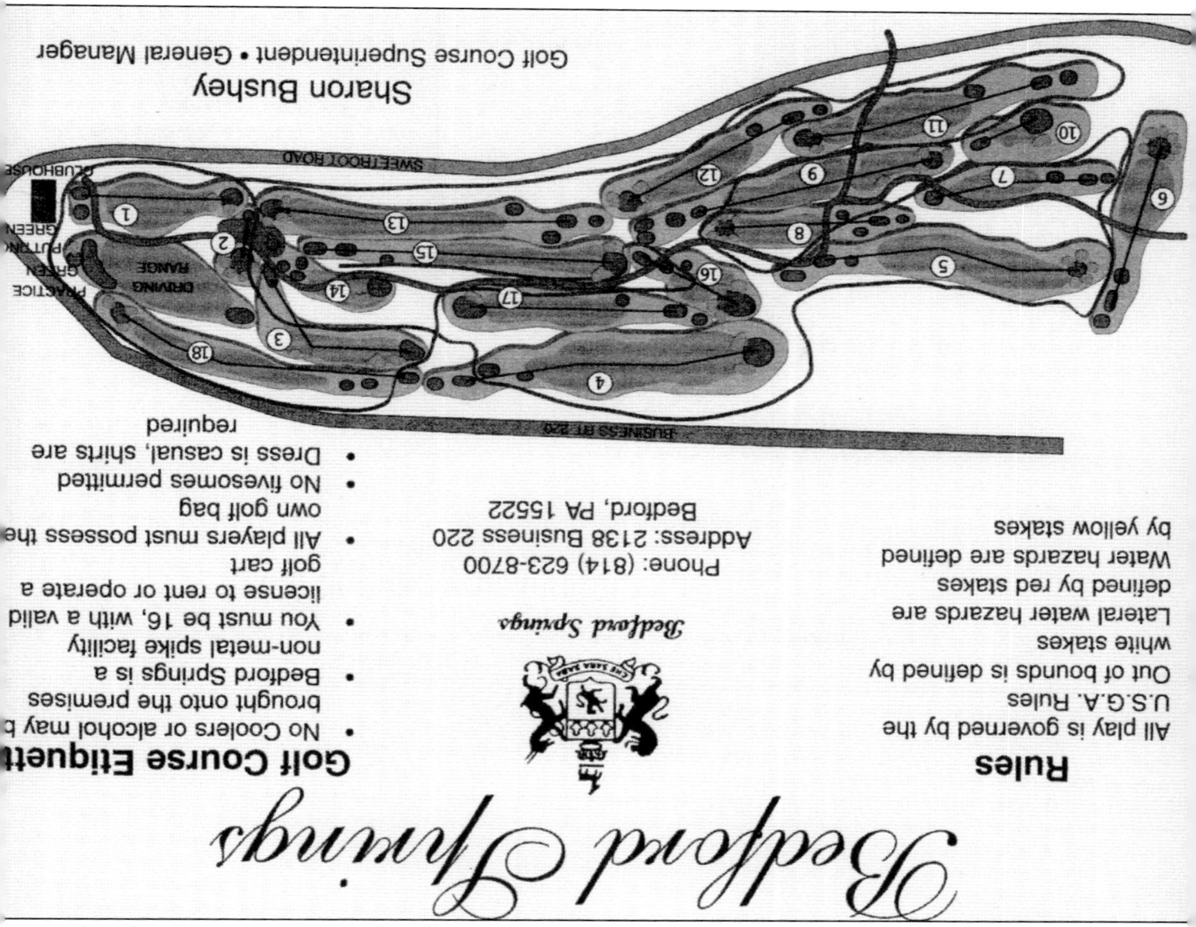

This plan from a c. 1980 brochure has been intentionally placed upside down to correspond with the plan to the left. In the 1980s, more changes were made to the golf course, as a close look at the plan shows. The 1912-era 17th and 18th holes were removed and replaced with a putting green and driving range (shown at the left of the plan), and two new holes were constructed. The hotel buildings would be beyond the far left of the plan.

From 2006 to 2007, the golf course at the Bedford Springs Hotel was restored. Forse Design Inc., golf course architects based in Pennsylvania, undertook the project. In reconstructing the golf course, the firm conducted studies of aerial photographs as well as historic research to restore the golf course to its 1923 Donald Ross design. This aerial photograph shows a portion of the course during its reconstruction.

This aerial shot is an overview of the golf course during its reconstruction. Today, the restored course at the Omni Bedford Springs Resort, or the "Old Course," is an award-winning golf course that is gaining in popularity once again. Two of the original holes and various course features from the 1890s still exist.

Five

Meeting the Demands of Modern Times

Before its 1950s resurgence as a modern resort, as can be seen in this c. 1950 photograph, the Bedford Springs Hotel had struggled its way through the Great Depression. It was then used during World War II by the US Navy as a radio training school followed by use as a facility to house detained Japanese diplomats from Berlin, Germany, after its fall. After renovations and modernizations following the war, the hotel regained its popularity as an upscale resort.

This c. 1930 photograph shows the hotel lobby in the Colonial Building. At the beginning of the Great Depression, the hotel property went into receivership. In 1940, Gardner Moore, a hotel manager from Washington, DC, started managing the Bedford Springs Hotel. His connections in Washington brought the US Navy and the State Department to the resort property during World War II.

The hotel dining room is shown in this c. 1930 photograph. During the Navy's use of the resort property from 1942 to 1944, the buildings were converted to training classes, lecture rooms, offices, and other facilities to accommodate the school. When the Japanese detainees arrived for their six-month stay in 1945, they were housed in the Barclay House up on the hill.

This full-sized, c. 1950 brochure highlights the amenities of the hotel. Following the war, Gardner Moore resumed management of the Bedford Springs Hotel in 1946 and helped return it to its former glory as an upscale resort property. He completed extensive renovations, which included upgrades to the nine-story Barclay House, and installed the outdoor pool on the front lawn. After renovations were complete, the Bedford Springs Hotel opened on a year-round basis in 1950. In the wintertime, sleigh rides, sledding, ice-skating, and tobogganing entertained guests, and annual Yule log celebrations and carol singing were held in the hotel. Red Oaks Lake was developed from the former Lake Caledonia for swimming, boating, and fishing.

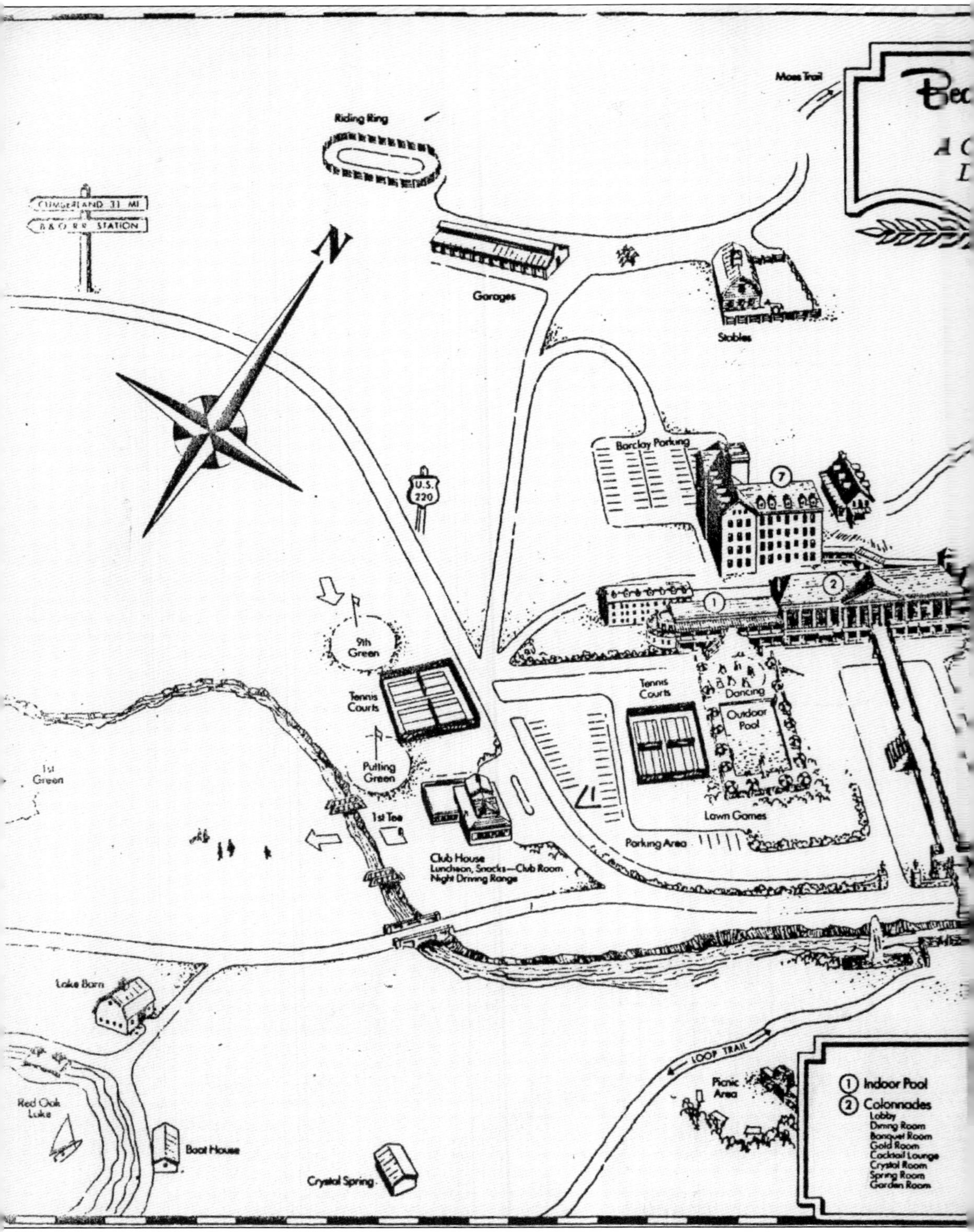
Moss Trail
Riding Ring
CUMBERLAND 31 MI
B & O R R STATION
N
Garages
Stables
U.S. 220
Barclay Parking
7
2
1
9th Green
Tennis Courts
Putting Green
1st Green
1st Tee
Tennis Courts
Dancing
Outdoor Pool
Lawn Games
Parking Area
Club House
Luncheon, Snacks—Club Room
Night Driving Range
Lake Barn
LOOP TRAIL
Picnic Area
Red Oak Lake
Boat House
Crystal Spring
1 Indoor Pool
2 Colonnades
Lobby
Dining Room
Banquet Room
Gold Room
Cocktail Lounge
Crystal Room
Spring Room
Garden Room

The Bedford Springs Hotel property is illustrated in this c. 1950 site plan. The plan shows the locations of the buildings and sports facilities in addition to the other resort features, such as the springs, the lake, the stream, the loop trail, and Shober's Run. According to the legend at the bottom, the Colonial Building was renamed the Colonnades.

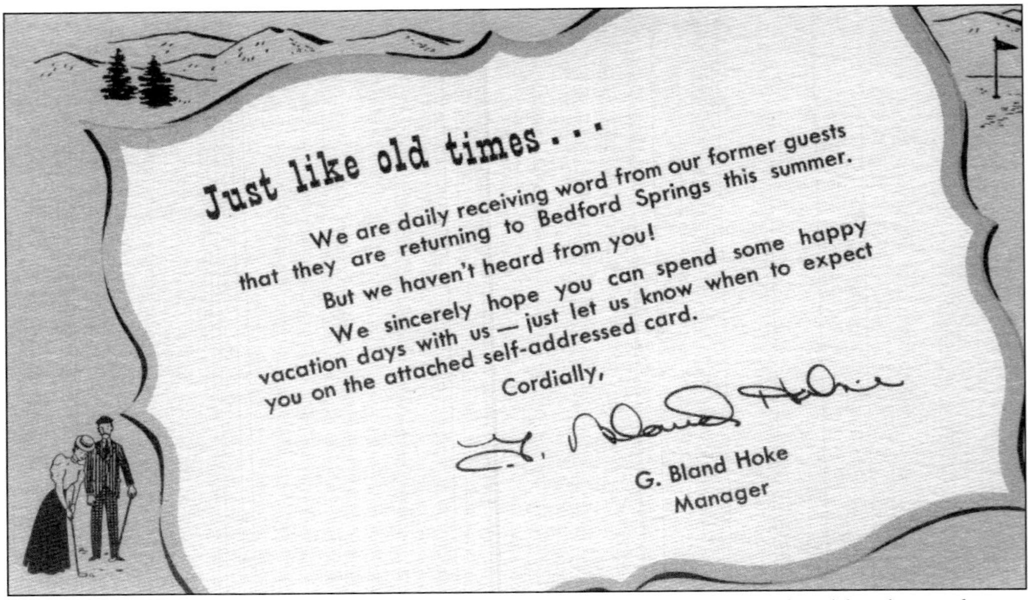

Just like old times . . .

We are daily receiving word from our former guests that they are returning to Bedford Springs this summer.

But we haven't heard from you!

We sincerely hope you can spend some happy vacation days with us — just let us know when to expect you on the attached self-addressed card.

Cordially,

G. Bland Hoke

G. Bland Hoke
Manager

G. Bland Hoke, manager of the hotel during the 1950s, sent out reminders like this to former resorters, reminding them to book their hotel rooms for the coming season.

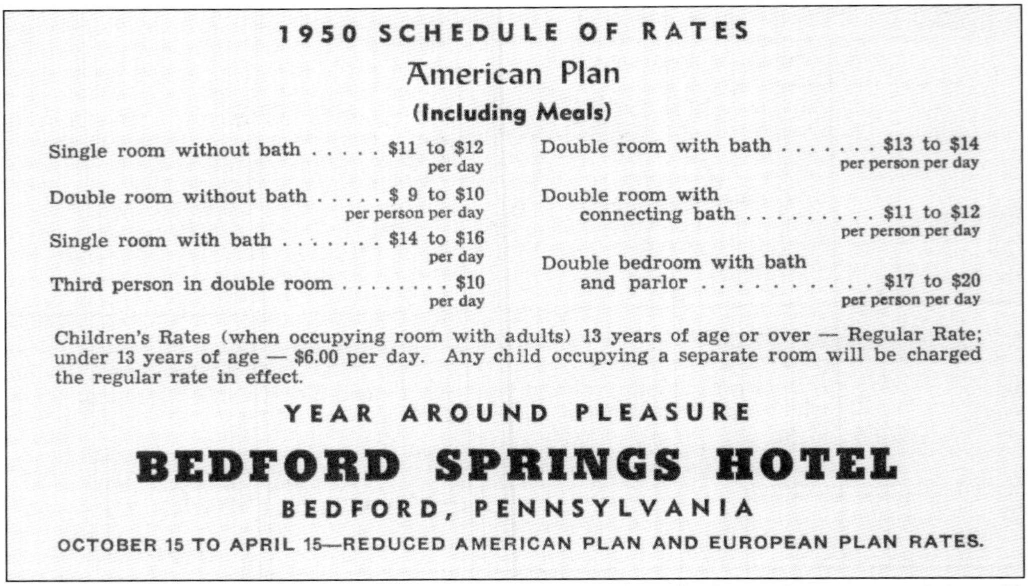

1950 SCHEDULE OF RATES

American Plan

(Including Meals)

Single room without bath	$11 to $12 per day	Double room with bath	$13 to $14 per person per day
Double room without bath	$ 9 to $10 per person per day	Double room with connecting bath	$11 to $12 per person per day
Single room with bath	$14 to $16 per day	Double bedroom with bath and parlor	$17 to $20 per person per day
Third person in double room	$10 per day		

Children's Rates (when occupying room with adults) 13 years of age or over — Regular Rate; under 13 years of age — $6.00 per day. Any child occupying a separate room will be charged the regular rate in effect.

YEAR AROUND PLEASURE

BEDFORD SPRINGS HOTEL

BEDFORD, PENNSYLVANIA

OCTOBER 15 TO APRIL 15—REDUCED AMERICAN PLAN AND EUROPEAN PLAN RATES.

Hotel rooms were available in different sizes, with or without baths, and costs ranged from $9 to $16 per night, with single rooms costing more. A double bedroom with an attached bath and parlor cost $ 17 to $20 per night. The hotel offered an American plan, with meals included in the price, but for those wanting a modified meal plan, a reduced American plan and European plan were also available.

In September 1962, former president Dwight D. Eisenhower and his wife, Mamie, visited the Bedford Springs Hotel for a Republican Party fundraiser for William Scranton. After staying at the hotel, the Eisenhowers went to Hershey, Pennsylvania, the following day for another event. Ronald Reagan visited the Bedford Springs Hotel. In 1975, prior to his 1980 election as president, Reagan gave a speech to the Maryland Chamber of Commerce at the Bedford Springs Hotel.

This c. 1950 photograph depicts the front of the hotel. In 1953, two physicians specializing in balneology conducted a study on the vanishing Pennsylvania spa resorts. They concluded that all but three of the original 75 mineral spas in the state had disappeared. Their article appeared in *Transactions and Studies of the College of Physicians*, and they hoped to "revive confidence in resort therapy" and see a "professional and popular attitude shift in the value of spa treatments."

The 1941 supper menu featured popular dishes of the day, including sirloin steak, broiled lamb chops, diced chicken à la king, creamed chipped beef, fried calf's liver, Welsh rarebit, and spaghetti. Wines by the bottle included domestic and imported ports, sherries, sauternes, burgundies, muscatel, and claret, ranging from $2.25 to $12 for a bottle. Cordials were sold for 60¢ to 70¢ each, long drinks ranged from 60¢ to $1, fizzes cost 60¢ to 70¢ each, and whiskies were sold for 70¢ each.

The 1980s were uncertain times for the Bedford Springs Hotel. The hotel's buildings were in disrepair, occupancy rates were low, and revenue was decreasing. Causing insult to injury to the faltering hotel was the unexpected flood in June 1983, which caused extensive damage to the buildings, tennis courts, and golf course. This photograph, taken in 1981 for the HABS/HAER recordation, shows the empty Colonial and Evitt Building. (Courtesy of the Library of Congress.)

The hotel stayed in operation, however, and the golf course was repaired. Events were still held at the hotel in the mid-1980s, such as an LPGA tournament and summer music festivals. After the summer season of 1987, the hotel was in bankruptcy and was forced to close. This photograph was taken on the front lawn in 1991, after the property was vacated. (Author's collection.)

Omni Hotels purchased the resort, and between 2005 and 2007, the company completed extensive renovations to the property. A large building was added to house the Springs Eternal Spa, designed by 3NORTH Architects of Richmond, Virginia, and the Barclay House was decreased in size from nine stories to three. The front lawn was cleared and extensively landscaped, as shown in this 2012 photograph. (Author's collection.)

The renovation was carried out with thoughtfulness and care to retain the significant buildings and features of the historic property while raising it to the standards of today's luxury resorts. The grand staircase and magnesia spring pavilion remained a focal point in front of the hotel, as shown in this 2012 photograph. When it was opened in 2007, the 2,200-acre Omni Bedford Springs Resort featured 216 guest rooms, a state-of-the-art conference center, a new 30,000-square-foot spa, and a restored golf course. (Author's collection.)

Bibliography

Blackburn, E. Howard. *History of Bedford and Somerset Counties, Pennsylvania, with Genealogical and Personal History*. New York: Lewis Publishing, 1906.

Defibaugh, William L. *The First Days of the Bedford Springs*. Bedford, PA: WLD, 2012.

Dr. John Anderson Papers (Manuscript Group 147). Pennsylvania State Archives, Harrisburg.

Fitch, William Edward, MD. *Mineral Waters of the United States and American Spas*. Philadelphia: Lea and Febiger, 1927.

———. Series of articles published for the Bedford Springs Resort for Health and Recreation. Bedford, PA: 1928.

Fonda, Sebastian L., MD. *Analysis of Sharon Waters, Schoharie County, Also of Avon, Richfield, and Bedford Mineral Waters*. New York: R. Craighead, 1860.

Library of Congress, Prints & Photographs Online Catalog; accessed March 2012. http:/www.loc.gov/pictures/.

Long, Steve. *Doubling Gap Center 1946–2006*. For Doubling Gap Churches of God, 2006.

Pennsylvania Railroad Company Passenger Department. *Summer Excursion Routes*. Philadelphia: Pennsylvania Railroad Company, 1888 and 1892.

Saxton, Cliff Jr. *Where Cares Refuse to Stay: The Story of Pennsylvania's White Sulphur Springs Hotel*. Northfield, MN: Loomis House, 2009.